TAX AND THE AMERICAN SLAVES

SHORT BUT TO THE POINT

by

◈ Sheron Beyers ◈

authorHOUSE™

1663 LIBERTY DRIVE, SUITE 200
BLOOMINGTON, INDIANA 47403
(800) 839-8640
WWW.AUTHORHOUSE.COM

First published by AuthorHouse 07/21/05

ISBN: 1-4208-5898-X (sc)

Library of Congress Control Number: 2005904715

Printed in the United States of America
Bloomington, Indiana

This book is printed on acid-free paper.

ACKNOWLEDGMENTS

I WISH TO THANK MY SISTER, DORIS HENDERSHOT, FOR keeping me informed on the politics of California.

I wish to thank The Winds Publishing Company and Jonathan Thompson for the article on the internet, (a must read) "Oklahoma Bombing Grand Jury Loses Credibility."

I wish to thank Bill Kurtis for his T V program on A & E, "American Justice"

I wish to thank the Biography channel for the program "Notorious"

I wish to thank Eric Jaffa of MOVE LEFT.COM for his piece on the internet regarding the supreme courts ruling on Eminent Domain. Kelo vs New London.

I wish to thank all the citizens who wrote letters to their editors voicing their opinions on the eminent domain ruling. You have voiced the opinions of the greater populace of the American people.

DEDICATION

This book is dedicated to all the American
TAXPAYERS
Past, Present and Future.

TABLE OF CONTENTS

‐ ‐ ‐ ‐ ‐ ‐ ‐ ‐ ‐

INTRODUCTION

— — — — — — — — — —

THIS BOOK IS ABOUT THE RUNAWAY TAXING SYSTEM IN America. We, the people, pay all the wages and benefits for every public employee in America, it is our tax dollars at work, that allow the government employee's to kill in Cold Blood, and never be held accountable.

It is our tax dollars that pay federal judges who, refuse to allow witnesses to testify, (Oklahoma City Bombing). It is our tax dollars that pay the entire justice system to allow district attorney's to do plea bargains, and judges, who, over-ride the sentencing of jurors.(Baby Sitter).

This about the many government cover-ups, and things they knew before-hand regarding terrorist activities in the U.S. (Sept.11)

The facts about the banks and credit card debt, and the legal loan sharking of the banking industry.

The Social Security Administration, and rules are different for different citizens. Why does the Federal Government own so much land? And the high taxation of State Governments.

Everything in the book is regarding the tax dollars we are paying to a government who cannot control it's own agencies, federal and state governments alike.

In America, you are always GUILTY, until you prove yourself innocent. (I.R.S. & Courts of Justice System)

CHAPTER ONE

THE BEGINNING

━ ━ ━ ━ ━ ━ ━ ━ ━

THE MAYFLOWER FINALLY REACHED PLYMOUTH ROCK, after a hazardous journey, and the pilgrims rejoiced. They believed they were finally free of the high taxes of England, and the laws of the King.

As the pilgrims progressed and formed the colonies they began making their own laws to live by. In 1765 the English parliament passed a stamp tax to be paid by the colonists, well this did not go over too well with the colonists, they refused to pay taxes to England.

In 1770, the British parliament declared war on the colonies as the British believed they should have full control of the New World, AMERICA. Hence came war and the Boston Massacre, where the British troops cared not who was killed, men, women, or the children. Ben Franklin was at this time in England trying to get the parliament to repeal the Stamp Tax against the colonies. England refused.

In 1773, the infamous Boston Tea Party showed the English government that the colonists were dead set against paying taxes to England. After the Tea Party, parliament repealed the tax.

Thanks to Ben Franklin and the bravery of the colonists for not backing down they did not become tax slaves to the King. It is so sad to know that those citizens, our forefathers, and Ben Franklin fought so hard against what we have today, I.R.S.

After England threw in the towel, (tea party did it) Franklin, Jefferson, Hancock, Adams, etc. began drawing up our constitution, and the BILL OF RIGHTS.

They also set forth the governing bodies, President, Vice President, Senate, and our House of Representatives. In the constitution these great men drew up we, the people, of this New World called America, they clearly stated there would not ever be an INCOME TAX to burden the citizens of The New World. AMERICA.

Thomas Jefferson may have had an incling of what was to come as he stated," There has to be a revolution at least every 200 yrs. or the government will become too big and consequently over power the people." EX-AMPLE-Federal Judges who over power the vote of the people (California's proposition 187 in the 1980's) I believe what he meant was not RIOTS, or not MILITIA GROUPS, (note here, possibility of militias as we so far, have the right to bear arms, thanks to the N.R.A. and all the conservative Americans) I believe what he meant was limited terms in all public offices.

Our Presidents have had limited terms for some years now, however, our Senators and Representatives, for the most part are LIFERS (State and Federal) We, the people, must limit the terms of any and all public office held in the U.S.A., City, County, State, and especially Federal. They should also be limited to no more than 2 terms. The way it has always been, we have had lifers, except George Washington who is to date the only President who did not go for the power of the office, since his decline to serve a third term, since then the Presidents we have elected only wanted the power of the office, as do our Senators and Representatives, and it is only the POWER of the office that cause all politicians to become LIFERS. The expense accounts, health insurance, raises whenever them deem it necessary, all out of taxpayer dollars.

We need new ideals and new blood in every aspect of our governing bodies. But, guess what, we have a big problem don't we? In order that we can change the terms of office we must VOTE the lifers out and until we can do so we cannot change it can we? Seeing as how they do all the voting in Congress, and it would have to be passed by Congress, unless we get the terms of office limited, we, the people, are screwed. And I believe Thomas Jefferson new this would happen. The revolution he was talking about depends on every American in the country, as we are the voters, and WE need to VOTE THE LIFERS OUT.

There are an awful lot of these lifetime politicians, Ted Kennedy for the very best example I can think of as he LOVES the LIMELIGHT, and always has. I have not figured out what is wrong with the voters of Mass. As Mr. Kennedy has been one of their State Senators for some 48 years now.(it must be PORK BARREL-ING) ? That's half a century, horrible, especially after the cover-up by the Federal Government and his brothers in Washington DC, and the agencies that was in charge during the CHAPPAQUIDDICK event. Anyone who thinks that was not a cover-up has rocks in his head for brains, and about everyone in America knows it. We will get to Government cover-ups later.

We know we must pay taxes, however, why an IN-COME TAX, and a high one at that? In 1862 president Lincoln needed an income tax to pay for the civil war, AS HE IS THE ONLY PRESIDENT WHO REFUSED TO PUT THE COUNTRY INTO DEBT. The French government (who by the way, saved us from the British) offered their help but he declined as it would have thrown the country into such hevy indebtedness. No wonder that is why he is know as the best President the United States ever had, and probably we ever will have. He levied a 3% tax on incomes between $600 and $10,000, and a 5% on incomes over $10,000. In 1867, 5 years later the citizens began to oppose the tax, (what we need to do today) so LO and BEHOLD, Congress cut the tax rate. In 1872, 10 years later, the government repealed the INCOME TAX as the civil war had obviously been paid for. In 1894, it was started again by the Wilson Tariff Act. In 1895 it was ruled UN-CON-STITUTIONAL by the Supreme Court. (We must have had some good supreme court judges at that time, unlike today) The income tax division was disbanded.

In 1909, President Taft, a Republican, recommended that congress propose a constitutional amendment (DAMN HIM FOREVER) to bring the income tax back. The controlling party in congress was at this time the DEMOCRATIC PARTY, and by DAMNED of course they passed it, AS THAT IS WHAT THE DEMOCRATIC PARTY HAS AND ALWAYS WILL STAND FOR, HIGHER TAXATION to burden the citizens, and by doing so, they DOOMED the American citizens into slavery, it seems forever. In 1918 the Revenue Act imposed a progressive income tax of up to 77 % and from that day forth it has only gotten worse in my opinion, as with the I.R.S. a citizen is GUILTY until he or she can prove otherwise, and this is not the only government institution that this holds true. (Another Chapter)

In 1942, another DEMOCRAT, President Franklin D. Roosevelt hailed the revenue act of 1942, 'THE GREATEST TAX BILL IN AMERICAN HISTORY' Congress had raised the income tax, I guess to pay for the war. Of course Roosevelt did not have to worry about any increases in the tax structure, as the Roosevelt's are and always have been Multi-millionaires, but the poor working stiffs are Shit-ON-A-Shingle aren't we? This is another good example of why we need to limit the terms of ALL public offices, as almost all of our politicians are already very wealthy, (have to be at the cost of running for office and this is another reason our system really sucks) so the I.R.S. is no big deal to them either, their idea is, "let the working class pay, we and the larger corporations have so many loop holes that the tax will not hurt us. I would like to repeat I believe this tax to be illegal and I will always believe that, as it was NEVER to happen to the citizens of the U.S.A., and the founding fathers protected us from this slavery in the constitution. Thanks to the RICH presidents and RICH politicians they have amended our constitution to the point that it is only beneficial to the wealthy, and any and all large corporations. (Oil Co., Drug manufacturers, etc. etc.) We, the average citizen, have been screwed over by I.R.S. our government, and now by our supreme court judges.

Will it never stop!!!!!

CHAPTER TWO

I.R.S. THE DICTATORSHIP

■ ■ ■ ■ ■ ■ ■ ■ ■

I .R.S. THE PARASITE THAT BLEED'S US DRY YEARLY, HAS so many employee's that the left hand of the agency does not know what the right hand is doing. I had and I.R.S. employee tell me once that the Ogden, Utah office couldn't find their ASS with both hands, if their life depended on it. I also know this to be a fact as I had to deal with that office several times. I believe that anyone who works for the I.R.S. is a TRAITOR to our forefathers who DID Guarantee that we would never pay an income tax, and I believe that the politicians who amended our constitution to force the people into a tax slavery are also TRAITOR'S to our forefathers and our constitution. Where in the HELL was our Supreme Court when this happened, asleep as usual probably, or paid off.

There was probably a lot of STUPID people in this country that thought it was pretty neat when Leona Hemsley, (I think that is her name), was caught by the DICTATORSHIP and had to pay an enormous amount

of back income taxes, well, I didn't think it was neat
at all, after all she and her husband worked for their
money and I doubt very much if any politician or I.R.S.
employee helped them earn one thin dime. And which
I.R.S.   Employees and politicians helped WILLIE
NELSON compose and sing all his songs? None of
those parasites helps any working stiff, they just keep
sucking our blood.

In a dictatorship, there is but one ruler, in the event
you do not know the meaning of the word dictatorship,
in Webster's college 2nd edition dictionary, it is as fol-
lows, 1. The position or office of a dictator. 2. A dictator's tenure of office; time that a dictator's rule last's.
3. A dictatorial government; state ruled by dictator. 4.
(This is the one that fit's I.R.S. to a tee) ABSOLUTE
POWER OR AUTHORITY.

If you have ever had any dealing's with the I.R.S.
you will understand EXACTLY what #4 means and
you must hate these trator's as much as I, and as every
American citizen does.

I feel so sorry for all the foreigners that are still coming to America, as they think we are a FREE people,
how mis-guided they are. They do not realize that the
American citizen never owns anything, we pay tax till
we die, get no help from our government in time of
need, and EVERYTHING is beginning to be against
the law.

Now, I ask you, are you free? Now, I tell you, NO,
your are not FREE. If the people of the U.S.A. were a
free people, we would not have the largest dictatorship

in the world in AMERICA would we? Our dictator is the INTERNAL REVENUE SERVICE and our problem is our own government WILL NOT STOP them our POLITICIANS damn sure won't even try to stop them, so what are we citizens to do? If we were not all so troubled and busy with our everyday lives, we could try to fight, and beat, the I.R.S. and FORCE the Federal Government to ABOLISH the slavery we are ALL under.

I have to wonder what the men and women of the Civil War, WW1, WW2, Korean War (police action) Vietnam War (police action) Gulf War #1, and now Gulf War #2 really were and presently fighting for, and I am sure there are a lot of them that feel the same way. They were supposed to be fighting for FREE-DOM of the other countries, but how can you fight for someone else's freedom, when you, yourself, are NOT free. The servicemen and women are forced to do this. FREEDOM as defined in Webster's 2nd college edition, 1. The state or quality of being free;esp., (a) exemption or liberation from the control of some other person of some arbitrary power;liberty;independence;thene) a being able of itself to CHOOSE or determine action freely (freedom of the will) g) ease of movement or performance;facility, etc. etc.etc. In plain ENGLISH we are not a free people.

In the United States of America, no person, man, woman, or child, owns a solitary item, maybe your clothing, IF they are cheap clothes, surely you cannot own a fur, or anything of value, because if you do, and you owe the I.R.S. any money, they will take it, so maybe, we don't even own our clothing. And guess what, the STATE government's picked right up on this dictatorship, and are just as bad as I.R.S., for heavens sake you better not be late in getting your taxes paid, or you will not have anything left to pay tax on.

I cannot believe that our government is trying so hard to get the communist countries to go to a democracy, as they must be just as free now as we, in the U.S.A. because we never own anything either, and all we do is work for the government. If your are a business owner, you do NOT OWN that business, no matter how large or how small the business is, you are strictly a manager of that business for the I.R.S. and the Fed., State, County, and City governments, all of them get a piece of your action, and if you don't give it, you lose the business and they wait, as some other fool will rush in.

Getting to the difference between a democracy and a republic. There is very little difference in the two, however, there is a difference. The U.S.A. was not to be a democracy, but rather a republic. Where in our Pledge of Allegiance do you see the WORD democracy? I cannot seem to find it anywhere.

Democracy, defined by Webster's dictionary; 1. Government in which the people hold the ruling power either directly or through elected representatives; rule by the ruled. 2. A country, state, etc. with such government. 3. Majority rule. 4. The principal of equality of rights, opportunity, and treatment, or the practice of this principal. 5. The common people, esp. as the wielders of political power.

Republic, defined by Webster's dictionary; 1. A state or nation in which the supreme power rests in all the citizens entitled to vote (the electorate) and is exercised by representatives elected, directly or indirectly, by them and responsible to them. 2. Any group whose members are regarded as having a certain equality or common aims, pursuits, etc. 3. a state or nation with a president as its titular head.

Take a good look at #2, now I ask you, when is the last time , that you can think of, has the democratic and the republican parties or politicians, had the same pursuits, or common aims, to benefit the citizens of the U.S.A., for as long as I have been alive 63 yrs., all they have ever done is fight. When they fight, we, the people, LOSE. They cannot agree on one damned thing, why? Because one or the other wants to be the BIG DOG.

The big difference between a democracy and a republic is that the majority always rules, no matter what, that means that if you are having a discussion with 5 or 6 people, and you, yourself, disagree with the others, whether you are right or wrong, and can even prove it, they will still win the argument, as majority rules.

In the case of I.R.S. this definitely is NOT the case, as they are always right, and you are always wrong. This is the reason they are a dictatorship, we are supposed to be innocent until proven guilty, according to the constitution, but, this is not so if the I.R.S. says you are guilty of a tax error, believe me you damned sure are, at least until you spend a small fortune on a lawyer or a C.P.A. to prove you are right. I've been down this road myself, and that's why I hate the I.R.S. so badly, they have cost me a lot of money, just like they cost Leona and Willie, and a hell of a lot more of the honest citizens in this country. I have yet to know when GOD died and turned our fate over to I.R.S.

Again I will say I.R.S. is the parasite of the citizens of America. If we did not have the parasite but instead, had a FLAT FED. SALES TAX @ 5% and NO more than that, not only would it help the government VASTLY, but the people as well. Everyone would pay what their means would allow. If you are a poor person and purchased a vehicle for $1000.00 you would pay your FED. TAX of 5% on that money. If you are a middle class person and bought a vehicle for $40,000.00 the same holds true, and if you are a wealthy person and bought a vehicle in the amount of $500,000.00 the same holds true. And this would stand true of everything that we , the people, shop for and buy. There is only two things that should NEVER be TAXED, and that is the FOOD we need for survival and existence and Medication when we are ill, that we must take to become well again. (At this time almost all states in the union tax both, food and medicines, and it should be illegal as hell)

The 5% Fed. Sales Tax would allow the citizens to have a pay, as you go, system and it would also help the government. Just think, it sure would be nice NOT to have that APRIL 15th dreadline wouldn't it? And the FED.'s would be raking in the sales tax daily. IT WOULD HELP US ALL.

Some Presidential candidates who has wanted very much to do exactly this, for one reason or another, did not get elected. SHAME, SHAME, they were the ones who wanted to help Americans. Personally I have felt this way since the 60's, where in the hell is everyone else. The liberals are always out in the north 40 somewhere, we know, but where in the hell have all you conservatives been?

Think of all the tax dollars that would be saved if we ABOLISHED the I.R.S. and that's not counting all the TREE's that it takes to keep up with the paperwork they change every year. It must take MILLIONS of $$$$$$$$ per year just to operate ONE office. The building, tapes, discs, file cabinets, desks, phones, computers, wages, benefits on top of wages, ETC. ETC. ETC. I believe the paper products and their BENEFITS alone would more than pay our NATIONAL DEBT. In the first year. With all the I.R.S. offices we have in this country I believe that if we abolished this OBSOLETE system the FEDERAL Government would not only be DEBT FREE, but would have a surplus at the end of the first year. What is wrong with our politicians in Washington D.C., and what is wrong with the UNITED STATES SUPREME COURT JUSTICES, who has allowed the STATE's to charge an INCOME TAX.? I'll tell you what's wrong, they just do not give a DAMN about the CITIZEN period, because if they did this would never have been, now would it?

Note: The one and only time the country was free of debt was during the Presidency of Andrew Jackson, 1829-1837

Tax any tax imposes a strain and a burden on the people. In the U.S.A. today all our taxes keep going up, Federal, State, County, and City. This tax increase yearly must be what is called , Cost of Living increases. We pay a hell of a price to be alive don't we?

To have a decent home we sure as hell do pay for it don't we? Property tax is extremely high all over the U.S. What I.R.S. doesn't take out of your earnings the State, County, and City Damned sure does. I was talking to a Professor from the University of Reno one day about taxation and I could hardly believe what he told me regarding taxes on a loaf of bread. It is taxed from the time the farmer starts his machinery to begin discing or plowing the ground to plant the seed for the grain, he pays the tax on the grain he buys to begin the growth, he pays tax on any and all fuel to plant then to harvest the grain, then it goes to the mills, they also pay tax on the same grain, etc. etc. etc. until you buy it. He said there is over 100 taxes placed on one loaf of bread by the time it is purchased at the grocery store. If this is the case, it stands to reason that everything in our country is taxed the same way. I have got to wonder why the U.S. Government is always running in the RED. Maybe it kind of explains how our politicians can give themselves raises. All our tax dollars must be going somewhere, besides our Military needs. Citizens wages for the most part seldom go up, unless a promotion gives one a raise, otherwise you are dead in the water. If you are fortunate enough to get a promotion, it usually only throws you into a higher TAX bracket and instead of bringing more of your check home, you bring less home, thanks to I.R.S.

Of course we do have an awful lot of citizens in this country who do not pay taxes. We the people, support them, and in a very good fashion. These are the people who are imprisoned for one reason or another, and the taxpayers of America pay dearly to keep them off the streets and in prison. We house them, clothe them, feed them, give them free medical, give them access to computers, libraries, etc. so they can learn more ways of how to break the law and get off by using the system. A few years ago there was a Sheriff in Arizona who had the right idea about men in prison, of course all the liberals and do-gooders sure as hell did not approve of it, but I thought it was great. He felt that a prisoner was not as good as our servicemen who were fighting for their country, however, they are sure as hell treated that way, ask any Vietnam Vet. He said a prison compound should amount to wooden barracks with army cots and no fringes, T.V., computers, etc. and they should have to work. They should have NO FRILLS. But the liberals in America seem to believe that rapists, murderers, child molesters, etc. etc. are better than our servicemen and women, let them sleep in foxholes in the rain, let them eat cold beans out of a can, let them die of exposure, whether from sun or cold, while they are defending America, but for HELL'S sake don't treat our murderers, rapists, or child molesters this way.

SHAME, SHAME, what in the HADES is wrong with these people, I will never understand. And on top of this, our service people all have to pay TAXES.

CHAPTER THREE

TAX AND THE AMERICAN TAXPAYER

— — — — — — — — —

THE PEOPLES OF EVERY COUNTRY MUST PAY TAXES, WHICH is what keeps their government running, however, the tax structure of the United States (Federal, State, County and City Taxes) quickly became like the tax structure of the other countries of the world. The American taxpayers have , at one time or another, helped many foreign countries in the world. After any disaster, be it hurricane, earthquake, volcanic eruption, or just re-build their country after a war. Every time a foreign country needs help, it is the American taxpayer that sends help.(Of course, we do not get the credit for it our Federal Government gets the credit.) We, the people, have never minded helping out, but don't you think it's about time that we began keeping these tax dollars at home to help our own people? We have many thousands of homeless that are every bit as poor and hungry as any that are overseas but I have yet to see our government help them, HAVE YOU? NO YOU HAVEN'T. Why doesn't the government take all our prisoners out of prison, put them on the FRONT LINES in war time (IRAQ) and let them fight FOR us for a change, and give the homeless the prisons to live in without guards, guns, or wardens, they would have very nice roofs over their heads, food, clothing, computers, T.V. libraries, etc. and the American people could actually feel pretty good about their-selves by actually helping a fellow citizen who needs help instead of a murderer, rapist, or child molester. (Charles Manson should have been sent to Iraq, but instead, he is living in a prison being taken care of by US, the tax-payer. He should have been put to death in the 60's)

You say welfare programs have helped, not hardly, the ones who really need don't get it, and the ones who have learned how to screw the system, do so and get by with it most of the time. Any female who remains on welfare for over 6 months and becomes pregnant during that time should be fixed so she cannot have any more children and be removed from the program. This would eliminate a lot of wasted tax dollars. The ones who really need the welfare programs or a food stamp program are treated like the scum of the earth by the government employees who work in these programs, and if you have anything you have to sell it before you can get any help. For the most part this is depending on what state you live in I think.

In 1988 my father had surgery at the age of 75, and he was completely disabled following the surgery, my mother asked for help from Medicare and the State of

Calif. So she could put him into a nursing home until he recuperated and she could care for him. (They were told they would have to sell their home, all but one car, (they had 2 cars, a 1966 Ford Ranchero and a 1975 Chrysler Cordova, real wealthy people huh?) and could not have any money in the bank, before the state or Medicare would help. The only money they had is what they had saved from their social security checks each month. But they did have their 24 x 60 foot mobile home paid for, and my mother said she would not sell it, she would try to care for my father herself. I was no help to her as I was living out of state, in Reno, Nev. however, I did drive every weekend home to Modesto to give her all the help I could. That's when I found out that Mom was actually in worse health than Dad. Mom was 71, 5'3" and weighed 96 lbs. The really bad thing is that they both had worked since they were very young, my Dad, since he was about 12 and my Mom, since she was about 14. They married, raised 3 children, paid their fair share of taxes during their productive years, and when my Mom needed just a small bit of help the State of Calif. And the Federal government both turned their backs on them. The burden of caring for my Father I believe contributed to my Mothers death on Sept. 23, 1990, after her death my Father went to live with my brother who cared for him until his death in 1992. This is only one story of fact, I believe there are an awful lot of the same stories in the U.S.A. I think that after our productive years of paying taxes, and when we begin getting to the point where we need help from the government that we paid all those taxes to we are treated like a pair of worn out boots, stuck on a fence post somewhere to fend for our-selves. This is a FACT, however, if you are a foreigner you sure as hell are treated a lot better. It is only the American Born Citizens who are treated this way. (Our government wonders why there are Militia groups all over the U.S.A., well this is only one reason why, the American taxpayers are mistreated by our government.)

The American taxpayer is more than likely feeding and clothing a large portion of the world population right now, we are the ones that are busting our buns every day, 6 days a week for a lot of us, so that we can pay those ILLEGAL INCOME TAXES, to not only give our politicians their raises when they deem it a necessity, but to bail out the countries of the world that need bailing out, thanks to their own governments taking advantage of it's peoples, and the GOOD OLE BOY'S in Washington D.C. and in the State Government's as well, caught on to this action a long time ago, that is why so many states began a State INCOME TAX. If the American people had not gotten so lazy, and so busy trying to earn a living for their families which , by the way, our politicians just absolutely love, as the people are not watching closely enough to what they are doing while in office. If the people had, had the time to pay attention to what was really going on the government could not have gotten away with so much, however , the only way the people can learn of such things is through our news media and the news media are ALL just a bunch of liberals, so the people never get the whole truth, only a bunch of propaganda. It would certainly be wonderful to have a news network for the conservative people, and give the real news, not just news to RAISE THE RATINGS, who the hell cares about ratings for news networks? It certainly is not the people who would like to get the real news, instead of propaganda bullshit.

The Social Security Administration has their problems as well as the I.R.S.. Another Gov't. Agency that is really bad. They not only are slow when it comes to paying benefits, but the same rules do not apply to everyone. If you are self employed you are only allowed to work 40 hours a month, but if you work for someone else you can work all the hours you want to. Does this make any sense,? NO it does not. A citizen is only allowed to earn X amount of dollars if we retire between the ages of 62-65, want to know why they do this, it's because the gov't is hoping that we will kick the bucket before we reach 65 and 4 months. With our children all raised they get to keep the money we have worked for, paid in for many years and they are also hoping that our spouse has passed away as well. Our FICA withholding will go to no one , only the Government.

We, as citizens should not be limited regarding hours or wages period. Our Gov't wants us to be flat broke all the time or to only be allowed to exist not to live life after retirement. If the S.S.A. Agency would allow people to earn more those people would be paying more into the program at least for as long as they work and keep earning money than at present they are allowed.

I, myself, fought with the S.S.A. for over a year as I was self-employed, was only allowed to work two hours a day five days a week, which I was able to do, and did, and they still refused my benefits. I had a partner and her and I paid ourselves by paychecks just like the employees. I turned all my paycheck stubs into them, my W-2 wage earnings to them and still got nothing. I sold my half of the business to my partner, proved that to them, to no avail. After the first 6 months of fighting with them I contacted my U.S. Representative, to no avail. I do not know if she did nothing, or S.S.A. was not about to allow me my benefits. But nothing changed for me. That was June 2004. After a year of this and getting nowhere, in Jan.2005, I contacted one of my U.S. Senator's office, Mike Enzi, and the lady that works there, Karen, told me this was not the first time this happened. She said she would definitely find out what was going on. I called her in the AM and that very afternoon she called me back and said that after talking to the local office she called somewhere else, another office, and she said they approved me while she was on the phone, I should be hearing from them with-in 2 weeks and if not please call her back. Well my good grief one day before the two weeks were up they finally paid me my benefits, full benefits for the entire year that had passed. I called Karen and thanked her very much, and told her, had she not pursed it, I do not believe I would have ever have received any of my benefits, at least not until fighting with them for another year, or until I turned 65 and 4 months, which by that time I could be DEAD and they wouldn't have to ever pay my benefits. That is exactly what they are counting on, that we die first. Cannot prove it , but there is no other reason for holding up benefits when you prove you are worthy. THE FRICKING GOVERNMENT, and GOVERNMENT EMPLOYEE'S. They all act like it is coming out of their own damn pockets.

How can our government justify sending BILLIONS of dollars to foreign countries for foreign civilians and turn around and treat us, the American taxpayer, like we are all crooks, outlaws, and the scum of the earth. This is exactly how we are treated by the employees who work for the gov't, be it Fed., State, County or City, but the Federal employees are by far the worst.

(Federal employees, have, and are allowed to, commit murder and get by with it.)

Some friends of mine were over the other day and we were discussing the S.S.A Diane was telling me that Terry (husband and wife) could tell me a story about the S.S.A. It seems that his parents are retired, in their late 70's, live in a very modest house, worth about $30,000.00 in Frannie , Wyoming. His father had surgery and his mother was unable to care for him, he had to go into a nursing home, Medicare would not pay for it, nor help, so they went to social security, and they told them that S.S.A. would help put him into a nursing home but, they would have to give up his S.S. check, she could keep her S.S. check, but they would also have to sign their home over to S.S.A., and upon their deaths the home would go to the gov't. These people, just like my own parents, (probably yours too) worked, raised a productive family, paid taxes their entire working live, but they are treated in the end worse than any murderer, rapist, etc. etc.

What is wrong with our government, when our elderly need help they must give up everything they own before they will receive any help from the government they paid taxes to their entire working lives. This is not only the Federal gov't. But also State gov't. I guess what we have to do in order to get gov't help is go out and commit a crime, go to prison, so we can be properly cared for, and our spouse won't lose everything we worked for. DOES THIS MAKE SENSE ? Yes and NO. They can send billions of dollars oversea's, care for murderer's, rapist's, child molester's, but they cannot care for our homeless or our elderly. Why don't they clean up their own back yard before helping the rest of the world, or telling the rest of the world how to live?

I have another friend who also has a horror story about the S.S.A. Her dad passed away in the early 80's, her mother, after some time, had met a fellow, who like herself, was drawing social security benefits, (again there is a problem) they wanted to marry but could not do so, if they got married they would only be allowed to receive her benefit of $900.00 per month as it was higher than his benefit of $800.00 per month. In their 70's now, they must live in SIN, thanks to our gov't. She was Morman, and the church ex-communicated her for living in sin. No person's can survive on $900.00 per month in the year 2005, especially the elderly, with having to buy prescription medication's, they are so damned expensive, just like an office visit to the doctor. They were given NO choice by the S.S.A. but to live in sin, as they can live on $1700.00 a month. We are SUPPOSED to be "ONE NATION" under GOD, however, our government has obviously thrown GOD away or so many of these agency actions would not happen. They say SEPARATE, GOD from STATE, well they have DAMNED SURE DONE THAT HAVE THEY NOT? They have also gone too far with it, like everything else, they got too carried away. Maybe we have a shit pot full of ATHEISTS in our government, it would seem so, since they have thrown GOD ALMIGHTY out of the S.S.A. It is no skin off of their noses if they force people to live in sin, is it ?

Social Security is just as dis-functional as the I.R.S. Just another gov't agency with employees that are better-than-thou. People are always saying, like-it-or-leave-it, well I really wish I could, financially I cannot do so. Our gov't is as much, or more so, just as corrupt as any in the world, with no one ever being held accountable. Gov't cover-ups following chapter. The stories of the above S.S. experience's repeat over and over again every day in the U.S. People WILL live in sin in order TO LIVE. God will not punish them, but rather, the one's who forced it onto them.

We, the taxpayers, are penalized for every improvement we make on our property, to our house, and even to a barn. If you build a fence, you are penalized, if you pour a patio or build a deck, you are penalized, if you build any kind of addition to your home, be it a garage or a bedroom for your mother-in-law, you are penalized, how are you penalized? By higher property taxation. In my case, I have been penalized for even putting down ceramic tile flooring inside my house, as the county agents for property tax evaluation look in the windows to see if they can see any improvements.

Building permits are another way of taxing I believe. With the building permit a contractor is supposed to be inspected, by a city or county building inspector. Well, to my knowledge, inspections are rarely done, and when they are done, it is normally done by some person who does not know what they are doing. The contractor's usually have to tell the inspector how things have to be. Case in point: I was in the process of building my restaurant in Nv., purchased brand new equipment and one piece of equipment was a steam table. The inspector came, and when he saw the steam table he said I had to put a drain hole in the bottom of it and have a sump sink underneath it. I called the health dept., got ahold of the head honcho, and she even said I would have to bring the description of the steam table to her. I called the place I had purchased it from, they took over all the paperwork on the table, then, as the inspector was waiting for an answer, the big shot called back, told him it was a steam table and does not come with a drain.

When a building permit sells for upwards of $2.00 per square foot, and this is for everything you build, added rooms, barns, homes, etc. I believe it is just another way of taxing us. The same holds true for the price of re-newing our drivers license, just another form of taxation.

We, the taxpayers, pay the wages for all the city, county, state, and federal employees, and we cannot afford health insurance (a lot of us) for ourselves, but we sure as hell can afford it for them through our taxes can't we?

I will continue to say, with the high taxation of our country, anyone after the age of 60, should never have to pay another tax, any tax. This will never happen, but that is the way it should be.

CHAPTER FOUR

GOVERNMENT COVER-UPS

━ ━ ━ ━ ━ ━ ━ ━

THERE HAVE BEEN COVER-UPS BY GOVERNMENT, BE IT FED. State, County, or City, since the beginning. As we become more advanced with the technology of today, 2005, it seems to get worse as time goes by.

A lot of cover-ups have happened in the past 50 years that I know about, and so do you, if you are old enough. We have the Kennedy's, Randy Weaver, David Koreish, and my personal opinion of Timothy McVey, right along with shootings in California to allow the state, by the voters, to pass Gun Control, in Alaska the same holds true for Joe Volger, and the hidden truth about our government hiring Nazi war criminals after WW2. In the state of Montana the people of Libbey, dying because of Asbestos mining, and lets not forget Ted Kenney's nephew Billy Smith, in Louisiana, during the Clinton administration, there are so many it is just un-real.

July 18, 1969, on a dark night, a lonely road, murder is about to happen. Ted Kennedy, who has NO drivers license, is DRUNK, is speeding, has a young lady in the vehicle with him. They have been to a party and after leaving the party Teddy must have made a wrong turn on the road somewhere, or did it on purpose, we will never know. A police officer, Huck, was behind them, Teddy got scared so he even speeded up faster to get the officer off his tail, which did happen. As a U.S. Senator, without a drivers license, and drunk to-boot, he was more concerned with his political career than safety. According to Huck's testimony, he only wanted to get Kennedy on the right road. Kennedy was on the right road alright, the road to murder. From the looks of things there were 2 houses only a short distance away after he went off of the bridge, and swam out of the water, leaving Mary Jo behind, in the car which was not totally submerged from the pictures, unless they pulled it up on shore, then took the pictures, but that is not important, what is important is the Kennedy boys were all athletic by all accounts in the news. What really should piss everyone off is the fact that he did not go for help, did not tell anyone for nine hours that Mary Jo was in the car. What in the HELL is wrong with this picture, and what in the HOLY HADES is wrong with the voters in Mass. For re-electing this jerk. According to the reports, Ted Kennedy was always a reckless driver, but he didn't have to worry about anything because his father had money and connections so he could just be a spoiled rich kid, which he was and still is. The people in Mass. That continue to re-elect a murderer is about 73%, but there are 27% of the population of Mass. That are wise enough not to vote for a person who left a young woman to die in a car, and who has become a lifetime politician, thanks to some real, in my opinion, stupid, non-caring liberal or rich voters. My hat goes off to the voters who did not vote for Ted Kennedy.

I believe he should be in prison, not in Wash. DC. AND I AM NOT THE ONLY ONE.

The Randy Weaver ordeal and the MURDER of his family is by far the worst thing that the gov't. Has ever done in my lifetime, that I am aware of. This atrocity is so great and NO one ever held accountable that it is still hard to believe. MURDER, by BATF, FBI and US MARSHALLS.

A man, his family, and a friend, all at home, on a quiet day in Ruby Ridge, Idaho. Little did they know that the agency's of the federal government was about to destroy the lives of them all.

Dogs began barking, not knowing the woods were filled with trespassers, (federal agents) Randy, his 13 year old son, and his friend, Kevin Harris, left the cabin, and began following the dogs, at this point gunfire came from the woods. Sammy Weaver, 13, turned and was running back to the house when he was SHOT IN THE BACK, by, according to the report, Marshall Cooper. Kevin Harris returned fire and shot and killed Marshall Degan, in self-defense.   The justice dept. says that it is impossible to know who shot first, well, if Sammy had already been shot in the back, I have to wonder why they cannot conclude who shot first. It seems pretty damned obvious who shot first, they shot the dog, then shot Sammy, at that point Kevin Harris returned fire. You do not have to be a rocket scientist to know that, just understand our gov't agencies, and their over-zealousness to do harm. After the shooting was over the marshals had to go recuperate, I guess they wore their-selves out. During this re-coop time they were able to get their stories straight. FBI snipers took up positions surrounding the cabin sometime after 5 pm on Aug. 22, 1992 and by 6:pm everyone in the cabin was dead or severely injured. Randy, Kevin, nor anyone else in that cabin fired a single shot at any agent. Shortly before 6pm, Randy, Kevin, and Sara Weaver 16 years of age, made a dash to the cabin where Sammy had fallen dead, an FBI agent began firing at them and hit Randy in the back. As the trio tried desperately to get back into the cabin, this same FBI sniper (real brave asshole) Lon Horiuchi shot again, this time at Vicky Weaver who was standing in the doorway holding her baby, his bullet went through a window in the door, hit Vicky in the head, instantly killing her, then struck Kevin in the chest. When all was said and done, Randy Weaver and Kevin Harris were, in a court of law in Idaho, found to be innocent, as they were protecting themselves, and trying to protect Randy's family.

To my knowledge, NO AGENT, was ever reprimanded, or tried for murder of innocent people, especially a 13 year old boy who was shot in the back, or a woman who was holding her baby, and a father who was trying to reach his slain son, who was also shot in the back. We sure do have some real Gutsy agents don't we.? What we really have is a pack, like wild dogs, if it was just one they would be too cowardly to face another alone.

Just how damned bad does it have to get before the American people will wake up and get the damned lifers out of political office so we can get some politicians in there who really do care about the American citizen, and start holding these agents accountable, for lying or for murder, and for everything in-between, if it is illegal.

We are supposed to have political action committee's who oversee the actions of our agencies. Well, I have to wonder what the hell they are doing except giving the President a bad time every time he wants to appoint someone for an office. Or if it not an appointment for someone, it is something else, like going after a mobster, or going after a genius like Bill Gates, because he has made so much money, and is so young, they cannot comprehend it. I believe they should get back to the real job at hand and come down on these agents for murder and mayhem.

The FBI, BATF, US Marshals, and all the rest of law enforcement, are nothing but trained killers that are trigger happy, and the Randy Weaver Family is a prime example of Agents who are trigger happy, instead of questioning the order to kill American Citizens who have done nothing to deserve dying for. There is a time in everyone's life when we have to question authority, the person giving the orders is not GOD, but just another human being, regardless of RANK, and our common sense tells us if things are right or wrong, and if it doesn't tell us then something is wrong with us. Education is worth a lot but not nearly what common sense is worth.

Waco, Texas is another story. Every religion in the world is a cult. A cult is, by definition, a system of religious worship or ritual. I, personally, do not believe the Fed.'s should have been involved at Waco, but, under the Clinton administration, we had none other than Janet Reno, right ? I think she was trying to show her ass when it came to Waco. I just really believe this was another time the federal government stuck their noses in where it did not belong. I believe that the Great State of Texas could have handled the situation far better than the trigger happy BATF agency and Janet Reno. Instead of killing all those men, women, and children, they could have done several things to prevent bloodshed. Why did they not set up a perimeter surrounding the compound, and sit still, cut off all utilities to the compound, let no one come or go, just like a prison, until they could reach an agreement with the obviously deranged David Koreish but no, they had to use force, and it did not matter who got killed. The agents knew he had firearms up the cabooska, so did they think he would begin killing his followers ? They probably did think that so here we go, the BATF thought that blowing the hell out of things would save the followers, right ? I don't think so, and Janet Reno sure as hell didn't think either, or just did not give a damn, about like the rest of the Clinton Administration.

Timothy McVey and his buddies. I will always think this was a government set-up and cover-up. The government allowed the news networks to take pictures of an axle that was supposedly from the van used to hide the fertilizer that supposedly blew up the federal building in Oklahoma City. I have a very good friend who is a restorer of vehicles, he said the axle they showed on TV was not even close to the axle of the van they said blew up the building. The van from the explosion was a Ford, the axle they showed was from a Chevy, or vise versa, but which ever, the axle from the explosion was not the axle the government says came from that vehicle. I also have a friend who is an explosives expert, and when this occurred John told me during our discussion of the bombing, that there is no way in hell a van with fertilizer blew up the building. According to John, the charges had to be set inside each room that blew out, because the building blew straight outward, not downward, which it would have done with explosives only on the ground Floor, parked at the curb, in front of the building.

THE SET-UP. The following is documentation from WINDS, taken off the internet. It states that four years before the bombing, the brother, of then Oklahoma Governor Frank Keating, wrote a book called the final Jihad. Martin Keating wrote this book in 1991, was not released until 1996.

Four years before the bombing Mr. Keating wrote of a terrorist network in Oklahoma with a central figure named Tom McVey. He tells of the terrorist's arrest based on a minor traffic violation by an unsuspecting highway patrolman. At the time Timothy McVeigh was apprehended it turns out just happened to be by an unsuspecting highway patrolman near Perry Oklahoma, only an hour and a half after the bombing. Televised news accounts for several hours thereafter were reporting the arrest of Thomas McVeigh. Was this a simple mistake, or an unplanned slip ? (author's opinion, it was the latter.)

Is this a bizarre, uncanny coincidence or is there some strange connection? The publicity notes which promote his book on an Internet site claim that Martin Keating is a master storyteller with unique access to government intelligence agencies and clandestine terrorist groups. His brother Frank is a former FBI agent and assistant secretary of the Treasury who supervised the Secret Service, U.S. Customs, and the B.A.T.F.

The notes further reveal that Keating was " introduced to the intelligence community through generations of family involvement. He knows intimate details of what the rest of us can only imagine. Armed with this firsthand knowledge...Keating accurately reveals what the highest government officials have known.

In 1991, Keating detailed beforehand in the book, The Final Jihad, a whole series of terrorist activities including the Oklahoma City bombing, the Arizona Amtrak derailment, the plane crash into the White House, the World Trade Center Bombing, and TWA flight 800. What does this say for all the government's denial of prior knowledge in the OKC bombing?

Keatings book corroborates the suspicions of many independent investigators who believe that high government officials had prior knowledge of the planned bombing.

Based on their past record, their strongest denials are tantamount to admission, which Keatings work only corroborates. This pattern of "denial equates admission" has been repeatedly demonstrated before the American people by their current president. (author, Clinton Administration)

THE GRAND JURY AND WITNESSES, GOV'T COVER-UP BEGINS, the immediate re-sponse to the bombing was the formation of a federal grand jury, it was organized to investigate the bombing and issue indictments against all perpetrators of the deadly terrorist attack.

Hoppy Heidelberg was a member of the original grand jury. Heidelberg told The Winds of his experience as a grand juror, the response of officials to his appeal for a comprehensive, independent investigation, and his removal from that position due to his insistence on conscientiously fulfilling his responsibilities.

He attempted to have specific witnesses called, to no avail. He said these witnesses would have substantiated whether the degree and pattern of damage to the Murrah building was comparable with a truck bomb.

"I tried to call the architect of the building because I needed to know how strong the columns were," said Heidelberg. " I needed to know what they could withstand in pounds per square inch pressure. I wanted a structural engineer to tell whether the building was built according to specs.

I wanted the engineer to analyze the column stumps and also the remaining columns to determine whether they could withstand that kind of pressure. Then I needed an explosives expert to tell me how many pounds per square inch 4800 pounds of ammonium nitrate produced at ground zero.

Then I needed a mathematician or the explosives expert, whoever could give me the formula for the dissipation of energy over distance. Then you have to plug in all the numbers and you can determine which, if any, of the columns could have been destroyed by a truck bomb."

Heidelberg says, " as a grand juror, I had every right to call any witness that was involved, any expert that I needed. I was prevented from doing all of that." He was further prohibited from showing the police a sketch of John Doe II to any of the witnesses. "They did not want me to pursue John Doe II at all," said the former juror.

It was his attempts to discover these fundamental facts which brought about Heidelberg's sudden removal from the grand jury. After repeated attempts to have these crucial experts, as witnesses, called he said, " I finally wrote the presiding judge a letter and told him. Once the judge had that letter he had a problem. If he had denied me those witnesses, then he would have been guilty of obstruction of justice, but if he had allowed me to have those witnesses, then I would have figured it out. So he had no choice but to kick me off; that way he could prevent either one of those (allowing the expert witness testimony or the obstruction of justice charge) from happening. That's how he got out from between his rock and his hard place."

Heidelberg said the judge didn't explain his dismissal, "He just wrote me a letter and said, you're out." Heidelberg said the threats and intimidation attempts were both overt and forceful. The base conduct of the FBI and federal officials toward Heidelberg is reminiscent of tactics used against some who have been labeled as Mr. Clinton's foes.

Following Heidelberg's dismissal, federal prosecutors proceeded to prevent every witness to any "John Does" from appearing before the fed. Grand jury. There exist more than twenty of such witnesses, yet not one was allowed to tell the grand jury what they saw, federal prosecutors prohibited those witnesses from being seen or heard by grand jurors.

Former Okla. State Rep. Charles Key stated that "the fed. Grand jury wanted to interview both the eye witnesses and the sketch artist who drew the John Doe composites but they were flatly refused by the federal 'authorities'. Clearly they were blatantly deprived of their basic constitutional rights as grand jurors. Why ? Just what is it that they are trying to accomplish? Or, perhaps more pointedly, just who are they trying to protect? And what all are they trying to hide?

With Heidelberg off the grand jury and other dissenting voices overwhelmed by official pressure and media silence, the indictment and conviction solely of McVeigh and Nichols went forward according to plan. This essentially assured that the one-man, one-bomb theory would prevail, suppressing all knowledge of wider involvement. (There is so much more to learn about regarding the corruption of the federal government and judge, right along with the justice dept. regarding the rail-road job by the federally's).

The Justice Dept., blatantly told ABC network executives not to go forward with a press story regarding prior knowledge of this incident. They said the American people, "could not handle the truth." (The people in government think we are all children and STUPID, this is their big mistake.)

Abner Mikva, a former White House council said, "Congress must move cautiously, the Justice Dept. Handles sensitive investigations...and many techniques must remain secret. If Chairman Hyde starts asking about all the dollars they spent in Oklahoma City, that can compromise some very, very delicate info.

Responding to Mikva's, "national security concerns," Cate McCauley of the Okla. Bombing Investigation Committee said, "I've heard this over and over again, 'No, you can't question certain people about things for national security reasons.' Well, if it's two guys and a Ryder truck, what are they so worried about.?

Cate McCauley tells of a woman named Tiffany Bible, an Emergency Medical Services employee who was on the scene within 5 minutes of the explosion. She was in the station south of the building, and she responded immediately. She saw BATF agents on the scene, in very clean black jump suits. They had not been in the building because they were clean. She noticed that because there was dust everywhere. She had a conversation after the 2nd bomb scare which occurred at 10:15 or 10:30. She was standing there with a BATF agent and a law enforcement person, by the federal courthouse on the south side, waiting for the all clear. They were saying, 'Yeah, there was a device strapped to a gas line, underneath the stairwell.' She distinctly remembers that statement because she had spent most of her time in that stairwell, trying to recover people. She said, " I could have gotten blown to kingdom come." She came forward , has since testified to the grand jury. It is that kind of testimony that is really hard to ignore.

Witnesses NOT ALLOWED. Per Pat Briley there were numerous witnesses who saw Timothy McVeigh with those who appeared to be Middle Eastern in Oklahoma City before the bombing and the day of the bombing. These witnesses were never called before the grand jury.

Jane Graham, witness to significant events which overturn the story officials constructed, she can hardly be construed to be an extremist or conspiracy nut, as so many others had been. At this time she is the local president of the American Federation of Government

Workers and an employee of the Dept. Of Housing and Urban Development (HUD). She was at work in the Murrah building at the time of the bombing. In a video affidavit, she gives a valid and detailed description of events she witnessed in the days prior to the bombing.

The Friday prior to the bombing Graham drove into the parking garage which is below ground level. She pulled into her parking spot and discovered three men in the basement. She noticed one of them was holding plans for the building. She saw that the other two had wire and some kind of putty-colored substance. She watched from her car as they were arguing . When they saw that she was watching them, the man who appeared to be in charge told the other two to put the materials away in a dirty, older model sedan. She wasn't able to see the car's license plate. Graham became uneasy when the three men began watching her. They wore street clothes and were not repairmen or telephone people, who would have been dressed in uniforms. She was wary about the incident, but lat it drop at the time. There were four others who also saw these three men the same day in the parking garage.

Graham also saw the two men who rushed past her on the morning of the bombing. They were coming out of a stairwell that could be accessed only from a " secured area" of the building. These men wore General Services Administration maintenance uniforms but she noticed they were not the regular maintenance men who were normally in the building. The coincidence of two GSA maintenance men being replaced on the same day seemed unlikely and she was puzzled she had no explanation for the strange people doing strange things in the federal building, that is, until 9:02 AM when the building was heavily damaged by two powerful explosions.

Graham told THE WINDS she felt the activities she had observed, the firsthand eyewitness testimony would be critical to a VALID, ABOVEBOARD grand jury investigation. She contacted D.A. Bob Macy's office to make a request for a presentation to the grand jury. After repeated futile attempts, it became obvious that the D.A.'s office was unyielding in its opposition to her testimony. The jurors were PREVENTED from hearing what she had to say.

The efforts to empanel the COUNTY grand jury began after the failure of the federal grand jury to act in an independent manner in determining what actually happened in the OKC bombing. Many of these same forces have come to bear upon the county grand jury, rendering it merely the instrument of powerful forces bent on covering up the truth.

The government's $50 million dollar investment to ensure that their "two boys and a Ryder truck" theory is not debunked has become transparent. The actual details of the deadly attack may not be available at this time, but as Cate McCauley said, "I think there was a network of people who had access to the inside of that building. Whether this is a bigger, badder set of terrorists than anything they have come up with yet, I don't know. WHO hired these people to do this ? That's what makes it so difficult, that you have, probably, layers between the free-lancers and the evil genius, as we tend to call him. Somebody got in that building, and the list narrows down when you consider means, motive, opportunity, and expertise. It is not something you walk off the street and do."

The past four pages have been taken off of an internet site, THE WINDS. If you want to learn more of the facts regarding the OKC bombing then please go to their website. You, like I, will be shocked.

I, after discussing the bombing with an explosives expert, and after reading the Winds website, am pretty well convinced, that Timothy McVeigh may have been involved, but,not the perpetrator. For all I know, he pissed off the government somehow, like Randy Weaver, and they set him up. It seems very strange to me that they put him to death so quickly, especially when you look at the prisoners who are on death row for years and years and years, and some like Charles Manson, who has been on death row for somewhere near 40 years.

There has to be a big reason why our government would not allow witness testimony, I will never be convinced that our own government was not involved someway. Otherwise they would have gotten to the bottom of it. This makes me remember how Hitler came to power in Germany, by terrorist activities, and our own government can and does, do whatever the hell they want to, and no one is ever held accountable, and no one ever stops them.

I am beginning to think that our oversight committees in Wash. DC are only doing things for the media coverage, to make the American people think they are on their toes, when all they really care about is getting re-elected. What a Fricking farce.

Joe Vogler , Fairbanks, Alaska. Joe was born on April 24, 1913 in Barnes, Kansas. He received his Law degree from Kansas at the age of 21. He went to Alaska in March of 1942 and worked for the Army of engineers at Ladd Air Field in Fairbanks until 1951 when he began mining on Homestake Creek. He spent 50 years "moving dirt" as a miner and real estate developer in interior Alaska.

Joe believed that Thomas Jefferson was the greatest political thinker who ever lived, and he believed that the federal government has overstepped their bounds, he challenged the federal government's practice of owning land outside the original limits of the U.S. Constitution. He believed that federal claims of land for parks and preserves is outside of the original intent of the framers of the Constitution and that the fed.'s have no right to own land in the western states except for "forts, arsenals, dockyards, and other needful government uses.

Joe loved Alaska and became very active in politics. He said, "Government is not the giver of rights; only God confers these to the people. People create government, giving it certain and limited powers. Only eternal vigilance by the people will confine government to its proper role" THE TRUTH COULD NOT HAVE BEEN SAID ANY BETTER.

Joe was a fighter for freedom, his own, and the freedom of his fellow man. When the federal government began taking the lands away from the people in Alaska, Joe was a bit irate, knowing it was not really legal, only politicians , who decided to make another amendment to the constitution to get more land for parks and preserves, which does not make it right, by any means.

Joe dis-trusted and hated the federal government so much that when his wife passed away he buried her in Canada.

Joe, one day, was on his tractor, going through a wooded area to get to his property on the other side, when all at once a helicopter came from overhead, he was told to leave the area, it was not for public use, the federal government owns this property and you are trespassing. Joe left the area, but it was not the end of it.

Joe began an ongoing war with the fed.'s. He knew they only wanted the lands because of the riches Alaska holds. The federal government wanted the Gold and the Oil of Alaska for the lower 48. The Alaskans were losing their freedoms just as the people of the lower 48 had lost theirs, years before. So Joe came up with a plan, get Alaska to secede from the union. He began working on this diligently. (I wish Wyoming would secede , as Yellowstone is in Wyoming)

A man Joe knew, I guess everyone in the area knew him, Manfred West, went to Joe's house and obviously killed him, for no reason that anyone knows about. At the age of 78, Joe was just beginning to get things accomplished for the people of Alaska, however, he did not know at what expense, his life.

As the battle continued between Joe and the government, things all at once began to happen. Joe was found DEAD. Manfred West was arrested and confessed that he killed Joe. After the murder, the U.N. sent notification that Iran would help Alaska secede from the union. Joe was killed before the news arrived.

Joe will always be my HERO, he stood up for the rights of the people and was murdered for it. I, like many, will always believe that Mr. West was paid to do the job, and I will let you come to your own conclusions as to WHO paid him.

Anyone who stands up for his rights is railroaded somehow, or ends up DEAD.

Author's note: Joe had contacted the United Nations for help in getting Alaska freed from the U.S.A.

In 1973, Joe got enough signatures on a petition to get Alaska seceded from the United States of America. Alaska would have been a fairly large country had he succeeded. Governing themselves, I believe they would have been mush better off, maybe they would not have had all the corruption that we now have in our government. It is too bad that someone did not "pick up the ball and run with it" after his murder.

Regarding the fight between Wyoming and the federal government, I can only say, we had it CRAMMED down our throats. The Wolves in Yellowstone.

The people in this great State did not want the wolves in the back yard, but that did not make any difference, they put them there in spite of the people. During the fight over this issue, I contacted a Professor at Wyoming State University, and we had quite the discussion, about the reason they got by with the wolf program. According to his philosophy, the people in the East think they own the West, since everyone migrated West from the East. The Easterners think that the West is their Playground, and they want to see Grizzly Bears, Moose, Elk, Deer, Black Bears, and Wolves, when they visit Wyoming, where the Deer and the Antelope Play.

The ranchers and the outfitters are not important to the federal government, it is only their lively hoods that are at stake, and the wolves are much more important. This is our government's mentality. They covered up the fact that they had been putting the wolf in Yellowstone for years before the Wolf Program was started.

I did not know the government was doing this, but my cousin, Mike Cook, (before he passed away) was a Park County Deputy Sheriff, he was in Yellowstone all the time, as he patrolled all over Park County. When I returned to Wyoming in 1990, after living in Nevada for 28 years, he was telling me how many times he had seen the wolves, almost every trip to Yellowstone, he either seen them or heard them. He said that he knew about the wolves for a long time, but never said anything as it would not go anywhere, the government would just say, " Oh, you must have seen a Coyote." Mike was born and raised in Northern Wyoming, has hunted since he was big enough to hold a rifle, and for any government official to tell him he did not know the difference between a Coyote and a Wolf, would have really pissed him off. But that is exactly what they have told numerous ranchers and outfitters, who damned well know better, but government keeps up the lies and bullshit.

When too many wolves were seen is when the government decided it was time to en-act the Wolf Program, at a cost of $30 million dollars, to the American taxpayers. When the wolves began leaving the Park, trying their best to get back to Canada, as a wolf, like a dog, does not ever lose his sense of direction, and as people began coming up with dead calves, sheep, pets, it was nothing to the government. The program continued, and still is, 2005.

The Wolves in Yellowstone was a government cover-up, until they produced and were seen by too many people.

Not only was there a cover-up regarding the wolves in Yellowstone, but it is my personal belief, (along with many others) that there was a big cover-up in the state of California in the 1980's in order to get Gun Control passed through the state legislation.

You may not remember, but there was a man who entered a fast food restaurant and began shooting innocent people, I believe he shot and killed four. That did not get the people too worked up, as there was almost always something disastrous happening in southern California, so, when that did not get everyone screaming for gun control, a few, I believe weeks later, then they had a freeway sniper. I cannot remember how many, if any, he shot. This incident did not get the gun control through either.

The two previous incidents happened in southern California.

Well, the government that wanted gun control, set up another plan. The federal government was trying it's best to get gun control legislation passed through congress. Thanks to the N.R.A. And millions of people who did not want any part of any kind of gun control fought it down.

I will always believe that it was the federal government who proceeded in the following incident, as they figured if they could get gun control in the state of Calif. The rest of the states would follow suit. And that is exactly what happened.

If you can picture a young man, 18 years of age, leaving Medford, Oregon to go to Stockton, Calif. Just to shoot up a school, then shoot himself, then you can see a lot better than I can.

This young man supposedly came into Stockton just to kill some children that were in a minority school. Then, supposedly, turned the rifle on himself.

This incident came over the news in Reno, I had grown up in Modesto, so I watched and listened with much interest to the broadcast. A minority school, with mostly Asian children, was attacked by a young man with a rifle, he shot and killed five children, then turned the gun on himself, so the news went. In my estimation, it is pretty hard to kill yourself with a rifle, like with a shotgun, a hand gun yes, rifle not easy. I watched the news the following day to catch more of the story, and lo-and-behold, not another word about anything, and nothing since. Cannot even find anything on the internet regarding this incident.

The government wanted gun control, tried killings in southern Calif. To no avail, so how is the best way to get the people's attention.? Go to the center of the state, Stockton is located damned near in the center of Calif. Hit a school, not just any school, but a school for minority children. Hire someone to do the HIT, then kill the hitman, The F.B.I. was on the scene immediately, and they are the ones who said the 18 year old shot himself. I don't believe it, and I never will believe it The state of California very shortly thereafter, had GUN CONTROL What does this tell you? It tells me, it was a set-up, and a cover-up.

It may be very hard for some folks to believe that the U.S. government could do such a terrible thing, but you must remember, to our government agencies (all) everyone is expendable, me, you and everyone in-between, man, woman, or child.The government will accomplish what ever task they see fit to do.

If you remember how Hitler got things accomplished in Germany, then this should not be very far from accurate to you. He was an officer in the German Army, had terrorists to terrorize the people, while at the same time, preached to the people, that if he were their leader, he would put a stop to the terror. He started everything, in order to become the Ruler of Germany. Our own government is no different, if they want something accomplished, they will, by hook-or-by-crook get it done. Go back and look at all the things that happened, and the people who were killed, during the Clinton Administration, especially the first four years. When he was elected for a second term, I just could not believe it. Liberals!!!

We are supposed to be able to have complete trust in our government, but how can we, when the government agents are allowed to KILL in COLD BLOOD. We are no different than the wildlife in Yellowstone, we are supposed to know what the government is doing, just like the Buffalo, Grizzly, Wolf, are supposed to know where the boundaries to Yellowstone are, and when they come up on a sign that reads, "leaving Yellowstone", they should read it I guess, and turn around and go back inside the Park.

The animals cannot read, and we cannot trust our own government, especially the government agencies.

Another government set-up in Idaho, Ron Nuckols, was set-up by the federal government by getting a former friend, Tammy Kaye, to have him get some pot for her, he told her he did not know where to get any

Marijuana, but she convinced him to try. He said he would try. Although Ron did not know where or how to get the pot, all at once he found someone who would deliver.

The government had already drove Ron and his family off of one ranch just outside a Nat. Park, in Idaho, so he bought another ranch outside Riggins, Idaho which lies just outside Hells Canyon National Recreation Area, well guess what, now the government wanted him off of that ranch as well. A good solid citizen, taxpayer, and probably a nice guy.

It could have only been an F.B.I. agent posing as a drug dealer who sold Ron one pound of Marijuana, so, Ron had the pot, he then gave or sold it to Tammy Kaye, then here comes the big boys. One man in particular Mike Merkley, , who was a Forest Ranger, was a big bad asshole who was always harassing Ron, and now they got him.

What was it about the Clinton Administration, always pushing the governments weight around, agents killing in cold blood, and decent citizens being harassed or shot by the B.A.T.F. Or the U.S. Marshalls, or the F.B.I., I believe to this day Bill Clinton should be charged and. punished for several things that took place during his reign.

In effect what happened to Ron is despicable, Mike Merkley knew of Tammy, and set up the whole fiasco with the feds. And prosecutor. The federal government wanted his ranch, so after they hired Tammy to set Ron up, they arrested him, and thanks to the good people in Idaho the plan did not work.

At the trial Tammy did not lie as the defense attorney asked her questions about the marijuana, and why she asked Ron to get it for her. She told the truth and it blew the federal government's case out of the water, the prosecutor must have had a little EGG on his face. It did not take the jury, (of great Idaho citizens) long to find Ron innocent, just like Randy Weaver, the citizens of the jury were able to see through the government's FOG.

I really do not know and can not even guess what drove the Clinton administration's zeal for such bloody and horrible action's. Was it because Hillary wanted, or because Bill wanted, to show the American people that just because they came from Arkansas, and had just defeated a great President in the election, that they, or at least one of them, would show the citizen's just what the government could do.

We, the people, had more disastrous happenings in the U.S.A. during the first four years of the Clinton Administration than during any other presidency that I know of.

We had the Randy Weaver cold blooded murders by the federal government.

We had the "blown-to-hell" Waco disaster.

We had the Oklahoma City bombing disaster (which feds had prior knowledge of)

We had people from the Clinton Administration shot, and called suicide's.

We had nothing but LIES from the Clinton's from the get-go.

How in hades Bill Clinton was elected for a second term of office I cannot even comprehend. And just how in the hell Hillary Clinton was elected as a U.S. Senator is even harder to comprehend, as far as I am concerned they are both about as worthless as the tits on a boar hog. They had Ted Kennedy behind them, so that must be the answer, and I also think he is just as worthless as the two Clinton.

Regarding the lands the federal government owns, I have gone to the internet to try and find out just how much land our National parks alone total. I cannot seem to get this accomplished as there are too many that will not give the square miles or the acreage. If I could get the acreage as in Yosemite it is easy, by dividing the acres by 640, which is a section, which is one square mile. However, not all sites even give us acreage, but of the ones I was able to get, it is beyond my comprehension how many square miles, just in National Parks, not counting Preserves, that belong to the Federal Government.

The lands belonging to the government is supposed to belong to the American Citizens, but guess what, they do not belong to us, otherwise, we would not have to pay enormous fees to go into our parks. We know that the roads must be cared for, and there must be rules to abide by, and without the Park Rangers , it would be a disaster in any park. However, the government wants too many parks and preserves, every time a President visits a beautiful place, it becomes a Nat. Park.

I totally know where Joe of Alaska was coming from, as the Federal Government has taken many square miles away from the Alaskan people in the name of Parks and Preserves. In Alaska alone there are, so far, 7 National Parks this does not include Preserves.

Yellowstone Park alone covers 3,472 sq. mi. or 2,221,773 acres. The National Parks are very pristine and we should save these areas, but to cram the wolves down the people's throat who live in the surrounding areas in assine. The outfitters who take out guided hunters, the ranchers who raise cattle and sheep, the people who live close to Yellowstone and have pets, dogs and cats, and small children, were ignored , as was 90% of everyone living in Wyoming. To me this was big government showing us, the pee-ons , who is BOSS.

If they were so intent to place wolves in Yellowstone, at a tremendous cost to the taxpayer, I wonder why they have not returned the Grizzly Bear to Yosemite, or to any other part of California, after all, the Grizzly is on the California State Flag, and on the endangered list. I think the reason the Fed.'s did not put the Grizzly back in Calif. Is because there are millions which populate that state, and the politicians are always and foremost, thinking of re-election. That is all they care about.

The population in Wyoming is right around 475,000, and the population of California is right around 30,000,000. I believe that is why there are no Grizzly Bears or any other animal crammed down the throats of Californians. Yosemite, being 1,190 square miles, is big enough for wolves and Grizzlies, but no, let the small percentage of the people in Wyoming put up with them, as there are not very many votes from that state. The same holds true of Alaska, with around 405,000 population. Back in the 70's there were not that many, when Joe was fighting for freedom from the U.S. Gov't. So, the government took the lands they wanted to take for Parks and Preserves, with Joe out of the way, I guess they had "clear sailing".

In the aftermath of the bloody Clinton administration's first 4 years, let us not ever forget Ruby Ridge, Waco, and the Oklahoma City Bombing.

Hitler learned of terrorism via the United States Federal Government through the history of our country and the way the our government treated the Native Americans. Our government thought that the Indians were inferior and wanted very badly to dispose of them altogether, there were very few Americans that stood up for the Native Americans. Our government, to this day, treat the Native Americans as tho they are inferior, that is why they still live on reservations that they do not wish to live on, as the Federal Government will forever keep their lands, and just pay them once a month, without asking where, and which lands belonged to them in the beginning, so they could be returned to those lands.

Hitler treated the Jews the same way, as he learned from our Government. There is no difference, only the method of torture and death is different. Our Government used guns and massacres to eliminate and Hitler used gas chambers.

The Clinton Administration probably took the lessons from Hitler, as his administration also began with terrorism, people who worked in the White House, come up dead and they called it suicide. The Ruby Ridge massacre, The Waco massacre, The Oklahoma City Bombing, and the fact that they could not put Tim McVeigh to death quick enough, especially when we have murderers on death row that stay there for years and years.

Watch out folks, because Hillary will be making a bid for the Presidency soon, and the good Lord best help us if she ever gets elected, as I believe the bloody massacres will begin all over again.

I believe that when government is responsible for murder, the murder is carried out by government agents, and the government agents are the ones who investigate the murder, federal judges preside over the courtrooms, so the government can cover it up and call it what they will.

I also believe that when John F. Kennedy was assassinated, it was do to J. Edgar Hoover and Lyndon B. Johnson and F.B.I. agents, and when the investigation began, it was by federal government agents and that is why the Warren Commission wouldn't or couldn't get to the truth   Regarding his assassination. When Jim Garrison got too close to the truth, they shut him up with threats. I also think that is the same scenario with Robert Kennedy's assassination. I believe this because Hoover could not stand the Kennedy boys and neither could Johnson. That why the offices were bugged by the F.B.I.

It is a sad day when the F.B.I. agents cannot resign instead of committing cold blooded murder, or become involved in a conspiracy to commit murder.

We, the populace, better get our heads out of the SAND.

CHAPTER FIVE

STATE TAXES

▬ ▬ ▬ ▬ ▬ ▬ ▬ ▬ ▬

THE STATES, FOR THE MOST PART, CHARGE HIGH TAXES, but the states that charge an income tax are really stretching it to the MAX. The peoples who live in a state that charge a state income tax are getting double whammied. In the United States there are only seven states that do not have an income tax. Alaska, Florida, Nevada, South Dakota, Texas, Washington, and Wyoming. If the population's of these states make a difference, which I cannot understand why it would, the following is the population of these states in 1988, which happens to come from a 1988 atlas I have, so I am sure they have changed somewhat, however, the only three states that I am sure changed dramatically is Alaska, Florida, and Nevada.

Alaska's population in 1988 was 401,851, Florida was 9,746,421, Nevada was 800,493, South Dakota was690,768, Texas was 14,227,574, Washington was 4,132,204, and Wyoming was 469,557.

We have various populations in the seven states who so not charge an income tax, so it cannot be that the other states, that do charge an income tax, have to do so. I think they just have too many state offices and state employee's. Just like the Federal government, too many employee's so instead of down sizing like any normal business has to do, they throw a higher tax burden on their citizens.

I will always believe that any INCOME TAX is as illegal as it can get, and for the states to ever be allowed to charge this heavy burden on it's citizen's is beyond my comprehension.

California is one of the best examples of high taxation I can think of right now, and that I really know anything about, as I was raised there. Could not wait to get out of that state, and with Nevada bordering it, I made a bee-line as soon as I was old enough, and since 1976 so have a lot more of California's taxpayers.

California, like many other states have high enough sales and property taxes, but in order to support all those state agencies and employee's, they, like the other states who charge an income tax, Burden the Hades, out of everyone who resides there.

I have a friend who lives in Dog Valley, an area just outside Verdi, Nev. But the state line between Calif. And Nev. Lies just outside of Verdi, so Mike lives in Calif. While he works in Reno, but he still has to pay state income tax to Calif. This does not make sense at all, he must pay personal property to Calif. But he should not be paying Calif. State Income Tax.

The following is a state by state tax structure, excluding gas, diesel, cigarette, taxes.

Estate tax in most of the states is only charged by the Federal government, however, there are states that do charge Estate taxes, rather than an inheritance tax. Please pay special attention to the states that do not charge tax on food, prescription and non-prescription drugs, and the high property taxes of some of the states that also have a state income tax.

ALABAMA- State income tax 2 % to 5 %
Sales tax 4 % to 12 % (prescription drugs ONLY exempt)
Property tax-personal property not taxed, real property varies by county.
Inheritance tax-NONE
Estate tax by Federal government.

ALASKA-State income tax-NONE
State sales tax-NONE   Local municipalities collect a sales tax of 1 % to 7 %
Property tax- varies by county or city.
Inheritance tax-NONE
Estate tax by Federal government

ARIZONA-State income tax 2.87 % to 5.04 %
State sales tax-varies from city or county from 5.6 % to 10.7 % (food and prescription drugs exempt)
Property tax-varies county to county, collected by

county assessors.
Inheritance tax-NONE
Estate tax by Federal government

ARKANSAS-State income tax 1 % to 7 %
  State sales tax-6 % to 11.5 % (prescription drugs
  ONLY exempt)
  Property taxes-varies, levied by counties,
  municipalities, schools.
  Inheritance tax-NONE
  Estate tax by Federal government

CALIFORNIA-State income tax-1 % to 9.3 %
  State sales tax-7.25 % to 8.75 % (food and
  prescription drugs exempt)
  Property tax-assessed at 100 % of full market
  value
  Inheritance tax-NONE
  Estate tax by state and Federal governments

COLORADO-State income tax-4.63 %
  State sales tax-2.9 % to 9.9 % (food and
  prescription drugs exempt)
  Property tax-varies, assessed by county assessors
  at a percentage of market value
  Inheritance tax-NONE   Estate tax by Federal
  government

CONNECTICUT-State income tax-3 % to 5 %
  State sales tax-6 % (food, non prescription and
  prescription drugs exempt
  Property tax-assessed at 70 % of fair market value

Inheritance tax-NONE as of 2005, will go to a limited estate tax
Estate tax by Federal government

DELAWARE-State income tax 2.2 % to 5.95 %
State sales tax-NONE
Property tax-Real property only, varies, county, city, municipalities
Inheritance tax-NONE, have a DEATH tax.
Federal government Estate tax

DISTRICT OF COLUMBIA-State income tax-5 % to 9.5 %
State sales tax-5.75 % (food, non prescription and prescription Drugs exempt)
Property tax-assessed at 100 % of market value
Inheritance tax-NONE
Federal government estate tax

FLORIDA-State income tax-NONE
State sales tax-6 % to 9.5 % (food , prescription, non-prescription drugs exempt)
Property tax-assessed at 100 % of market value
Inheritance tax-NONE
Federal Estate Tax

GEORGIA-State income tax 1 % to 6 %
State sales tax-4 % to 7 % (food, prescription drugs exempt)
Property tax-varies greatly
Inheritance tax-NONE
Federal Estate Tax

HAWAII-State income tax-1.4 % to 8.25 %
  State sales tax-4 % (prescription drugs ONLY
  exempt)
  Property tax-100 % of fair market value
  Inheritance tax-NONE
  Federal Estate Tax

IDAHO-State income tax-1.6 % to 7.8 %
  State sales tax-6 % to 9 % (prescription drugs
  ONLY exempt)
  Property tax-assessed at 100 % of full market value
  Inheritance tax-NONE
  Federal Estate Tax

ILLINOIS-State income tax-3 % flat rate
  State sales tax-6.25 % to 8.5 % (1 % on qualifying
  food, non and prescription drugs,
  Medical appliances)
  Property tax-33.33 % of market value, farmlands
  taxed on ability to earn income,
  Cook County is completely different, single
  residence taxed at 16 %
  Inheritance tax-NONE
  Federal Estate Tax

At this time I would like to bring your attention to the states sales tax (the first percentage No.) And the cities and counties sales tax, which is the second percentage number.

INDIANA-State income tax 3.4 % Flat Rate
  State sales tax-6 % (food and prescription drugs
  exempt)

Property tax-Real and personal property taxed at
100 % of full market value
Inheritance tax-1 % to 10 %, based on market
value
Federal Estate Tax

IOWA-State income tax-0.36 % to 8.98 %
State sales tax-5 % to 7 % (food and prescription
drugs exempt)
Property tax-assessed at 100 % of full market
value
Inheritance tax-1 % to 15 %
Federal Estate Tax

KANSAS-State income tax 3.5 % to 6.45 %
State sales tax-5.3 % to 8.3 % (prescription drugs
ONLY exempt)
Property tax- 100 % of fair market value
Inheritance tax-10 % up to $100,000, 15 % above
$200,000
Federal Estate Tax

KENTUCKY-State income tax 2 % to 6 %
State sales tax-6 % (food, prescription drugs
exempt)
Property tax-real property tax rate is 13.6 cents
per each $100.00 of assessed Value.(Real property
is 100 % of market value) confusing, yes!
Inheritance tax-varies (probably because of the
way property is taxed)
Federal Estate Tax

LOUISIANA-State income tax 2 % to 6 %
State sales tax-4 % (3.8 % tax on electric, water utility, stream)
(political sub-divisions may levy taxes up to 10.75 %)
NOTHING IS EXEMPT FROM SALES TAXES
Property tax-10 % of full market value
Inheritance tax-NONE
Federal Estate Tax

MAINE-State income tax 2 % to 8.5 %
State sales tax-5 % (food, prescription drugs exempt)
Property tax-subject to local as well as state, based 100 % of assessed value
Inheritance tax-NONE
Federal Estate Tax

MARYLAND-State income tax 2 % to 4.75 % cities and counties income tax 1.25 % to 3.15 %
State sales tax-5 % (food, non and prescription drugs exempt)
Property tax-100 % of full market value
Inheritance tax-Relatives are exempt, non relative is levied at a 10 % rate
Federal Estate Tax

MASSACHUSETTS- State Income Tax 5.3%
State sales Tax 5% (food, prescription drugs exempt)
Property Tax- varies greatly

Inheritance Tax-NONE
Federal Estate Tax

MICHIGAN-State Income Tax 3.9% Cities are
    allowed to charge an income tax as well
    State Sales Tax-6% (food, prescription drugs
    exempt) Home heating fuels 4%
    Property Tax-50% of fair market value
    Inheritance Tax-NONE
    Federal Estate Tax

MINNESOTA-State Income Tax 5.35 % to 7.85 %
    State Sales Tax-6.5 % Beer, Liquor, Wine 9%
    (cities and counties another 1 %)
    (Food, clothing, non-prescription, prescription
    drugs exempt)
    Property Tax-100% of assessed value
    Inheritance Tax-NONE
    Federal Estate Tax

MISSISSIPPI-State Income Tax 3% to 5%
    State Sales Tax-7% to 10% NOTHING IS
    EXEMPT
    Property Tax-15 % of assessed value with 30%
    assessed on motor vehicle value
    Inheritance Tax-NONE
    Federal Estate Tax

MISSOURI-State Income Tax 1.5 % to 6%
    State Sales Tax-4.22 % (prescription drugs
    exempt) food is taxed at 1.225 %
    Property Tax-Residential 19 % of fair market

value, Personal from 5 % to 33.3 %
Inheritance Tax-NONE
Federal Estate Tax

MONTANA-State Income Tax 2 % to 11 %
State Sales Tax-NONE (lodging tax 3 %, vehicle rentals 4 %)
Property Tax-100% of all real and personal property of assessed value
Residential property may receive a 32 % exemption, if filed for
Inheritance Tax-NONE
Federal Estate Tax

NEBRASKA-State Income Tax 2.56 % to 6.84 %
State Sales Tax-5 % to 6.84 % (food, prescription drugs exempt)
Property Tax-100% of full market value
Inheritance Tax-varies, collected at county level
Estate Tax-12 % to 16.8 %
Federal Estate Tax

NEVADA-State Income Tax NONE
State Sales Tax-6.5 % to 7.25 % (food, prescription drugs exempt)
Property Tax-35 % of assessed value
Inheritance Tax-NONE
Federal Estate Tax

NEW HAMPSHIRE - State income tax 5 %
State sales tax-NONE (8 % tax levied on lodging and restaurant meals)

(7 % on two way communications)
Property tax-100 % of assessed value
Inheritance tax-18 %
Federal Estate Tax

NEW JERSEY- State income tax 1.4 % to 8.97 %
State sales tax-6 % (food, clothing, footwear, non
and prescription drugs Exempt)
Property tax-varies, collected on the local level
Inheritance tax-varies on percentage
Federal Estate Tax

NEW MEXICO- State income tax 1.7 % to 6.8 %
State sales tax-5 % to 7.1875 % (qualifying food,
prescription drugs, medical Expense exempt)
Property tax-all is taxed, real and personal at one
third of market value
Inheritance tax-NONE
Federal Estate Tax

NEW YORK- State income tax-1.7 % to 7.7 %
State sales tax-4.25 % to 8.30 % (food, non and
prescription drugs exempt)
Property tax-real property only taxed at 100 % of
market value
Inheritance tax-NONE
Federal Estate Tax

NORTH CAROLINA-State income tax 6 % to 8.25 %
State sales tax-4.5 % to 7.5 % (2 % tax on food by
the counties)
(prescription drugs, medical equip. exempt

Property tax-real and personal at 100 % of
appraised value
Inheritance tax-NONE
Federal Estate Tax

NORTH DAKOTA-State income tax 2.1 % to 5.54 %
State sales tax-5 % to 7.5 % (food, prescription
drugs exempt)
(6 % lodging tax-7 % alcoholic beverage tax)
Property tax-real property subject to tax by state,
county, townships and Municipalities, percentages
varies
Inheritance tax-repealed in 1927, replaced with
estate tax
Federal Estate Tax

OHIO-State income tax-0.743 % to 7.5 %
State sales tax-6 % to 8 % (food, prescription
drugs, telephone service, newspapers, Magazine
subscriptions exempt)
Property tax-35 % of assessed value
Inheritance tax-NONE
Estate tax is levied by state as well as the Federal
Estate Tax

OKLAHOMA-State income tax-0.5 % to 6.65 %
State sales tax-4.5 %-counties add 2 %, cities add
4.25 %
(prescription drugs ONLY exempt)
Property tax-real property is taxed at 11 % and
13.5 % of fair market value
Inheritance tax-NONE

Estate tax levied by state as well as the Federal
Estate Tax

OREGON-State income tax-5 % to 9 %
State sale tax-NONE
Property tax-set by counties, varies
Inheritance tax-varies
Estate tax is levied by state as well as the Federal
Estate Tax

PENNSYLVANIA-State income tax- 3.07 % flat rate
State sales tax-6 % to 7 % (food, clothing, non
and prescription drugs, textbooks, heating fuels
exempt)
Property tax-levied by local governments, it
cannot exceed 30 mills of the Assessed value (a
mill is one tenth of one cent)
Inheritance tax-varies
Federal Estate Tax

RHODE ISLAND-State income tax-25 % of federal
taxable income
State sales tax-7 % (food, some clothing, precious
metal bullion, some Burial related items, non and
prescription drugs exempt)
Property tax-assessed and collected by local
jurisdictions, varies
Inheritance tax-NONE (Rhode Island has a very
different kind of tax going)
Estate tax is levied by state as well as the Federal
Estate Tax

SOUTH CAROLINA-State income tax 2.5 % to 7 %
   State sales tax-5 % to 7 % (prescription drugs
   ONLY exempt) Senior Citizens 85 and older pay a
   4 % sales tax,(real big break
   Huh, wonder if the state can afford it)
   Property tax-assessed and collected by local
   governments, varies
   Inheritance tax-NONE
   Federal Estate Tax

SOUTH DAKOTA-State income tax-NONE
   State sales tax-4 % (prescription drugs ONLY
   exempt)
   Cities have the right to charge additional sales
   taxes, state Has some rebates for 65 and older if
   you qualify
   Property tax-85 % of full market value
   Inheritance tax-NONE
   Federal Estate Tax

TENNESSEE-State income tax-NONE, rather a 6 %
   tax levied on stock dividends, interest from Bonds
   and other obligations
   State sales tax-7 % (prescription drugs ONLY
   exempt)
   6 % levied on food and food   ingredients (another
   real big break)
   Counties and cities may add 1.5 % to 2.75 % tax
   levies above the State levy
   Property tax-25 % of fair market value
   Inheritance tax-5.5 % to 9.5 % (this is sure not a

surprise is it ?)
Federal Estate Tax

TEXAS-State income tax-NONE
State sales tax-6.25 % to 8.25 % (food, non and
prescription drugs exempt)
Property tax-assessed by local governments,
percentage varies
Inheritance tax-NONE
Federal Estate Tax

UTAH-State income tax-2.3 % to 7 %
State sales tax-4.75 % to 6.35 % (prescription
drugs ONLY exempt, however a 2 %
Only tax residential utilities)
Property tax-100 % of fair market value
Inheritance tax-NONE
Federal Estate Tax

VERMONT-State income tax-3.6 % to 9.5 %
State sales tax-6 % to 7 % (food, medical items,
equipment and fuel, residential
Fuel and electric, clothing and shoes of $110.00 or
less, Non and prescription drugs are exempt)
Property tax-varies
Inheritance tax-NONE
Federal Estate Tax

NOTE: Every state in the Union should take a good
look at Vermont's tax exemptions

VIRGINIA-State income tax-2 % to 5.75 %
State sales tax-4.5 % (non and prescription drugs

ONLY exempt)
4 % tax on food as of 3/05, food tax to decrease to
3.5 % on 7/05
Will go down to 3 % on 7/06 and 2.5 % on 7/07
(wonder if they can Afford it too)
Property tax-100 % of full market value
Inheritance tax-NONE
Federal Estate Tax

WASHINGTON-State income tax-NONE
State sales tax-6.5 % to 8.5 % (food and
prescription drugs exempt)
Property tax-100 % of full market value
Inheritance tax-replaced by an Estate tax in 1982
Federal Estate Tax

WEST VIRGINIA-State income tax-3 % to 6.5 %
State sales tax-6 % (prescription drugs ONLY
exempt)
Property tax-varies, collected by counties
Inheritance tax-NONE
Federal Estate Tax

WISCONSIN-State income tax4.6 % to 6.75 %
State sales tax-5.5 % (food, prescription drugs
exempt)
Property tax-varies greatly
Inheritance tax-NONE
Estate tax is levied by the state as well as the
Federal Estate Tax

WYOMING-State income tax-NONE
  State sales tax-4 % to 6 % (prescription drugs
  ONLY exempt)
  2 % to 4 % added for lodging tax
  Property tax-assessed by counties, cannot exceed
  1.2 % of assessed value For cities and towns the
  rate cannot exceed 0.8 %
  Inheritance tax-NONE
  Federal Estate Tax

The populations of the states can all be found on the internet, if you want to figure out just how damned high your taxes really are to supply the agencies and the their employees for state governments I think you can do so, eliminating the schools, police and fire departments, which we need, however, in the city where I live we have more police per capita than anywhere in the U.S.A. I live in Cody, Wyoming, a small town with a huge drug problem, but our police are more concerned with school children buying cigarettes and smoking, and people visiting a local saloon than they are about the big problem, DRUGS. This could very well be the same all over America, as D.U.I.'s bring in a hell of a lot of money to the cities and the counties, plus, if a person gets caught enough times, they go to prison, become felon's, and cannot own a gun.

Regarding high state taxation, the state of California really comes to mind, but I am sure there are other states that also have very high taxation, but in the 1980's the California taxpayers had, had enough. Proposition 187 made it to the ballot, despite the federal government, state politicians, the opinion making elites, intellectuals, Canadian commentator David Frum, Washington neocon William Kristol, Cesar V. Conda of the Alexis de Tocqueville Institution, The Heritage Foundation,The Cato Institute, The Manhattan Institute, government employees, teachers unions, labor unions, big business, civil rights lobbies, public interest law firms, doctors, government hospital employees, big universities, Jack Kemp, Bill Bennett, and the media.

Despite all the opposition, the underfunded, politically inexperienced grassroots activists got enough names on a petition to get proposition 187 on the vote ballot. The citizens of California passed the proposition, they were fed up with the welfare of illegal immigrants, public housing, medical services, food stamps, government schools, all of which the California taxpayer was paying for. Education for the illegal children comprised 7 % of the states total student population at a cost of $2 billion a year for the taxpayers. The health care costs ran $1 billion a year for the taxpayers, welfare to single mothers $54 million a year for the taxpayers, subsidies to single mothers scheduled to reach $1 billion by the end of the decade.

Governor Pete Wilson tried to end this problem at the state level, but, in violation of California's rights, the federal government was forcing state taxpayers to pay up, whether they liked it or not. After Governor Wilson had taken out full page ads in the Washington Post, to give the taxpayers of California a break, to no avail of course, the taxpayers took the matter into their into own hands, and got prop. 187 on the ballot. At this point, they were smeared, called every name in the book, but did not falter. They also scared the hell out of the politicians, and all the rest of the nin-com-poops that were set totally against prop.187.

Any of the, quote, high mucky-mucks, that fought against prop. 187, were doing it for some kind of financial gain, from the WELFARE STATE.

The federal government was so stressed out over the prop. Passing, they had a federal judge in L.A. to override the vote by the people. At this point, had he been successful in overturning the vote, it would most definitely be Government TYRANNY, and this is actually what we live with every day, government tyranny.

I must say that since the Clinton administration has gotten out of office, the tyranny has not been super bad, at least we don't have federal agents killing in cold blood, like back then.

If the prop. 187 is going to continue and grow, it will depend on every voters tenacity, with independent minds and loud voices. As Teddy Roosevelt said, tyranny must never return, so walk softly and carry a big stick. He is another president that would literally shit-little-green-apples, if he were here today, 3-2005.

By walking softly and carrying a big stick, our vote is our big stick, seeing as how we, the average citizen, could not stand up to the might of our military, as the colonists did when they stood up to Britain.

The voters passed another proposition in California that really shook things up, it was prop.13. With extremely high property taxes, too many people were having to sell their homes just because they could not pay the property tax. Instead of the bureaucracies downsizing they continued to raise property tax, to the point it was, in my opinion, tyranny upon the taxpayers. California is still above the average state, when it comes to taxation.

The voters passed another prop. In California, that shook the shit out of things again. Prop. 215, now this has been an on-going battle with the Feds. The selling of marijuana legally for medicinal purposes, and to allow a person to grow a very limited amount for their personal medical needs. Well, here comes the feds, trying to overturn the vote of the citizens once again, D.E.A. agents, enter the picture, tearing out plants, storm-trooping through the state as tho everyone was a mass murderer, normal for a federal government asshole agent. The Tyranny in this case again is the Federal government.

Thanks to the taxpayers in the state of California, a lot of the states have, somewhat, lowered property taxes, and some of the states have also legalized marijuana for medicinal purposes. If the people's vote does not matter when it comes to things like prop.'s 187, 13, and 215, then I believe with all my heart, we must have a revolution in this country, against the federal government's agencies, and force the government, by vote, to cut these agencies down to size. I believe our federal government has gotten so big and un-ruly that when our constitution says "This government is a government for the people, by the people" then why don't the feds butt out. They have become such tyrants, and they wonder why such few citizens vote, well the reason people don't vote is because we the, (paeons) see what the feds do even when we do pass a law, by the voting power, either a federal judge tries to overturn our vote, or the storm-troopers are sent in, by our tyrannical federal government.

When the citizens vote no longer means anything, and the Supreme Court Judges, or any kind of federal interference, overturns the voting public, then this country has become nothing but a communistic country, and our presidents are always telling us about trying to rid the world of communism, and if this is the way we, the voters, are treated by the federal government, then you tell me, what is the difference ? There is none. When the States lose their power, we have certainly lost ours as well, as we are the citizens, and the voters, in the states, and Washington D.C. is NOT a state. What Washington D.C. is, is full of lifetime politicians like Ted Kennedy, who don't give a damn about the normal hard working citizen, except at re-election time, and that is just about the way it is for all the lifers in Congress.

We must set term limits for all of them, or kiss our ass goodbye, we must get I.R.S. abolished and go to a flat fed. Sales tax of no more than 5 % period, with no ammendent that can change it.

I believe that what we need in the U.S.A., is all of the militia groups to get together and stop buying arsenal items for some kind of warfare practice, but rather, join forces and start a taxation revolt across America. If the militia groups really want to help the citizens of our country, then they should organize, put the weapons down, form a group that can lead the people to revolt against taxes. We need leaders, and we need to stop the re-election of lifetime politicians at the state and federal levels, this is the one thing that must be done, and if it not done, then I guess it will be up to the GOD ALMIGHTY, to get something done.

I have said it before and will say it again, AFTER 60 years of age, we should never have to pay another tax of ANY KIND.

Too many states tax us on food, clothing, footwear, non prescription drugs, have property taxes that are so high, seniors have to sell their homes, and possibly everything else of value just to get by.

Social Security helps, and would help a hell of a lot more, if it wasn't for high taxation. What the feds don't get the states do, and the reason we are taxed to the point of rediculous, is because our state and federal governments have not learned how to DOWNSIZE. There is not a business in the world, and yes, government is a business, that could run a deficit like the governments do. If a business cannot pay their bank loans, or for that matter, any of their bills, they either close up shop, or file bankruptsy. Not so with governments, they raise the taxes and run in the RED, why? Because they are afraid to downsize, we have too many F.B.I., U.S. Marshalls, (I have not figured out yet why we need both agencies, the F.B.I. should be shit-canned all together, and keep the original, U.S. Marshalls.) The C.I.A. could really be downsized, and the be-damned B.A.T.F. should be downsized drastically. All the B.A.T.F. agents are, are government cold blooded killers, and the federally storm troopers.

We pay taxes, taxes, taxes, just to keep a government going that is non-accountable for it's actions. We, the people, need leaders to help fight this tax battle.

CHAPTER SIX

D.U.I.'S AND GUN CONTROL

— — — — — — — — —

YOU ARE PROBABLY ASKING, WHAT HAS A DUI (DRIVING under the influence) have to do with gun control? PLENTY.

There are an awful lot of folks who think we should have gun control, but I beg to differ with them. Our 2nd amendment is extremely necessary for our well being, as a country. Our military is extremely necessary for our well being, and together we can and have defended this country.

In 1951, I was 9 years old, the Korean war was all over the news broadcasts that my parents listened to on the radio. I was scared to death that we would be invaded and all be killed, a child of 9 or 10 and older and younger get scared when they hear things like this on news broadcasts.

I asked my mother one day if we were going to be bombed and killed, and asked her what if they invaded us, what would happen? Are they coming to kill us, I'm scared? Thanks to my mother's wisdom, she set my mind at ease. The first thing she said was, " Sheron, you know all the guns your father has? Well just about every household in this country has more than your father, so if the Koreans were to try to invade us they would have a great big fight on their hands, between the army and the citizens they would not stand a chance, and they know it. That is why we have never been invaded, we are allowed by our constitution to keep and bear arms to protect ourselves, and God will keep us from harm."

The children of today are no different than I was. They are scared to death over war on T.V. Without our firearms, they would be justified in being scared to death. Any idiot who cannot understand the necessity of the 2nd amendment should realize that without it, we could be in deep do-do.

Now we come to dui's across America. Every state has a different set of rules, in some states, if you get 3 dui's in 5 years you go to prison, in other states it is 3 in 7 years, some states are more lenient, 3 in 10 years, but you do not have to be an alcoholic to get a dui, but rather just have 2 or 3 drinks socially with friends in a bar. The cops watch the bars like vultures, as that is where the cities and counties and states make so much money.

Say a person gets 3 dui's in the 10 year span, has to go to prison, bingo, gun control without legislation. Felons cannot own a gun, so with this happening all over America, in every city and county, gun control and dui's are definitely attached to each other.

Defense attorneys are getting very wealthy over the dui's given out by cops. If, in this country they do not want anyone to drink and drive, maybe they should begin prohibition again, but the states and the feds cannot do that now can they? Look at all that revenue they would lose, and the gun control without legislation would and could not happen.

The federal as well as the state government's, city and county governments, are getting so much revenue off of the sales of liquor, beer, and wine and let me add cigarettes, that there will never be a prohibition against it again, they could not afford it, with the taxes on these items, plus the dui's they are really raking it in.

The dui's should not carry a prison term unless a drunk driver should kill someone in a vehicular accident, then throw that person in prison, but the average citizen who is only stopping in a bar for a social drink with fellow workers, should never be sent to prison, fines, if caught over the legal limit, yes, but not prison.

The legal limit has been dropped, first in California, to .08 and of course, the other states followed suit. MADD wants a zero tolerance, well I have to wonder what the lady who started the MADD program got when she got her dui, which was only on the TV news once that I could find.

When a federal judge, Thompson, was pulled over in Reno, Nv. The police officers immediately put him into a motel and tried to cover it up, but thanks to a good newspaper reporter from the Reno Gazette, the story came out. This is typical of all high mucky mucks, they do not pay the same price as us paeons.

If the truth were known, the high mucky mucks, drink as much or more alcoholic beverages than the average citizen but they, nor the cops who get good and drunk, do not have to worry about the problem, as someone will always be there to cover it up.

How little the law cares, about a family, when it goes after the woman or man, who has stopped at a bar, sometimes not to drink, but rather, to meet with someone regarding business. This exact thing happened in Reno, on So. Wells street, in the 1970's. A man from Washington, came to Reno to meet with a business associate, the bar they met in served lunch, they both only drank cokes, had their lunch, finished their business, and left. The man who was from Washington, walked to his car, as soon as he got in and started the car, here comes a boy in blue, they argued, the man told him he had just had a luncheon with a business associate and they drank nothing but coke, the little boy in blue arrested him for drunk in or about a vehicle. After the arrest, the man demanded a blood test, right then, Washoe Med. Center was just down the street, they took him down there, and he came back negative of any alcohol in his system period. When the man got back to Washington, he filed suit against R.P.D.

This is only one example of how gung-ho the police everywhere are when it comes to a bar they naturally assume everyone is shit-faced, they pile up all the dui's they can, do you suppose they have to meet a quota? Probably so, that's why they give rewards to people to call dui's in this is how they got gun control in England, turning neighbor against neighbor, for their guns.

The dui issue also is a driver's license issue, you lose your license to drive if convicted of a dui. In most states, you lose them for 6 months, if you refuse to take a breath test or a blood test, if you take the tests and are convicted, first offense, you usually lose the license for 1 year. In some cases you can get a license to drive to work and back, and that is all. Awfully white of the state isn't it,? But on a first offense, they sure don't want to lose any tax revenue do they?

When I lived in Nv. I contacted my state representative regarding the driver's license of a truck driver, the C.D.L. I recommended that a truck driver be issued 2 sets of licenses, a residential license, and a CDL license. This should be done for everyone who drives a company vehicle, as if the driver stops after work and has a beer or two with working buddies, gets pulled over, gets a dui, they could take his CDL if he was in the company vehicle, however, if he was in his private auto, with his wife, they should only take his resident license, so it does not interfere with his livelihood. Well, that did not even get an answer.

When I moved to Cody, Wy. I was still on the subject of the drivers license, as it seems so unfair to me. The best example I can give you is this scenario, A truck driver, long line, or local, parks his truck at the yard, gets in his private vehicle, goes home, showers, shaves, and wants to take his wife out to dinner. They get in the car, drive to a restaurant, have to wait to be seated, go to the bar, have a couple of drinks, get to the table, order wine with dinner, are enjoying being together without the children. They leave , go to the car, and on the way home, have a fender bender, someone has bumped them in the rear, no damage is done, but they must wait for a police officer to get to the scene. The officer arrives, thinks he smells alcohol on the guy's breath, gives him a stupid test, saying alfabet backwards, he fails, he is arrested and jailed, he is convicted, and loses his CDL license, by losing his CDL license he has just lost his livelihood. After months of trying to find a decent paying job and cannot, he and his wife, due to stress and financial problems, file for a divorce. By losing a CDL license, that should have been a resident license as he was not driving the truck, but his personal car, because of this he lost everything dear to him.

I also contacted a Wy. State representative regarding this matter, did not get to first base, just like Nv. What is wrong with the politicians, do they not care what the outcome can be for a family that depends on that CDL license?

A drivers license is supposed to be a privilege, and I guess it was in 1915, as there were so many people still on horseback and using wagons, but since I was born 1942, a drivers license has been a necessity. The only reason the country still calls it a privilege is because you have to pay the state every 4 or 5 years to get another one, and if you do anything wrong while driving they take it away from you. Another way for the government to keep control over the citizens, it is called MONEY and CONTROL.

Regardless of the reason, anyone who drives a company vehicle, of any kind, should be able to have private resident license, as well as a company vehicle license. The company license should never be revoked unless he is in the company vehicle, when something bad happens.

The drivers license is the most important thing to America's working public, and even to those who do not have to work but still have to run errands, buying groceries, going to the cleaners, taking and picking up school children, going to PTA meetings, going to a doctor or dentist, etc. etc..

I wish we could all go back to the horse and buggy days myself, what with the price of gasoline today being over $2.00 a gallon, and probably going to go higher. Another thing about the horse is they don't interfere with the ozone layer.

If the drivers license is not a necessity then why is drivers education taught in our schools.?

The trucking industry keeps America moving, and that is why I say that the CDL is the most important license in America, so why can't our politicians and our state governments understand that, of all people, the truck driver needs 2 licenses, a private license and a CDL (work license). I believe they do understand, they just don't give a damn, hell, it's no skin off their noses, they get paid whether people lose their livelihood or not.

Maybe the American people should go back to the horse and buggy days, at least a horse always found his way home, and never had a wreck getting there either, now wouldn't that piss our oil companies and OPEC off? Being feasible, that cannot happen, we will just continue being used and fined by our government, and be at the mercy of big oil companies.

CHAPTER SEVEN

THE AMERICAN JUSTICE SYSTEM

▬ ▬ ▬ ▬ ▬ ▬ ▬ ▬ ▬

THE FIRST THING I WOULD LIKE TO SAY IS, HOW IN THE hell does the celebrities get by with making a MOCKERY out of the justice system? It is so sickening to have seen what happened in the O.J. Simpson trial, and the mockery of the police following him for miles and miles down a freeway before they ever done anything, why, had that been any ordinary citizen, the cops would not have hesitated to block the vehicle, freeway or not, gun in hand or not, the cops would have been gung-ho to stop the vehicle. This is PROOF that the wealthy and well known are treated differently, than the average paeons, which we are as far as the powers to be are concerned.

Now we have another prime example of wealth in the courtroom, Michael Jackson, who has waned sickness not once but twice, while being in court, once in 1993, and now in 2005. How does this wealthy celebrity get by with wearing pajamas into the courtroom?

Because he is a celebrity, that's how. Any ordinary citizen, anywhere in America, would never have been allowed to do this. And why is it that his back pain seems to come and go with indictments?

In our justice system, you are GUILTY, until such time you can prove yourself innocent, the cops are allowed to lie to you in hopes of getting a confession, and are so gung-ho to catch a perpetrator, that they do not care if you are innocent or not, the chief, captain, and police commissioner have to look good for the media. The media is one of the largest problems when it comes to the justice system, not all reporters are assholes, but a hell of a lot of them are. You, if you happen to be a paeon, are tried in the media, way before you even enter a courtroom. A prime example of this is the media's role in the Central Park Jogger case in New York City. The media, tried and convicted, in their newspapers and TV commentaries, 5 very young black boys. Did they do this because the boys were black, or was it because the victim was a prominent white woman? I believe it was for both reasons. After they had served their sentences, for assault and rape, were released, the man who committed the crime, confessed while in prison himself. Now the boys, who are men now, are suing the city of New York for wrongful imprisonment, so now the word is out that they are suing "just for the money". Well I don't blame them, when the cops, while interrogating them, lied to one and then another of the boys, and after hours and hours of this action by the cops, they confessed. The prosecutor was no better than the cops in this matter, as she was showing pictures of the crime scene to a 14 year old boy, with police markers on the scene, just so he would know where the crime was committed. Before this was done, none of the boys knew where the crime took place. HOORAY, for the cops and prosecutors regarding this matter right? BULL-SHIT, the prosecutor as well as the cops who interrogated these young boys, should have to face a wrongful action, and be held accountable for their most rediculous methods, and serve the same amount of time in prison as these innocent boys had to serve, this is the only way our justice system will ever be fair to us all. Lies by cops and prosecutors in order to get a confession is bull-shit. And because of the media, these boys did not stand a chance for a fair trial. Now, had they been celebrities the outcome would have been much different, the media would have been on their side of things, and not have convicted them in the press.

Accountability is the one thing the judicial system does not have. The police all too often, when a crime is committed, just want to hurry up and find a perpetrator, and because of this, there are probably a lot of innocent people in jail, if they were held accountable for lying and forcing confessions, by having to serve prison time theirselves, this would certainly cease and the paeons would have justice, as most of us, cannot afford to hire a lawyer that costs $500.00 an hour, or more, to defend us, much less, like OJ Simpson, have 5 or 6 of these high rolling lawyers at the same time. I believe that the justice system should change drastically, limit the defendent to one attorney, and limit the prosecutor to one prosecutor, instead of the taxpayers paying for 2 or 3 prosecutors, and let the defending lawyer and the prosecutor fight it out between each other instead of 5 or 6 defense lawyers against 2 or 3 prosecutors. And make them all accountable for any and all lies, lawyers and prosecutors.

No one, regardless of how wealthy, should be able to have more than one attorney at a time, this is a big in-justice to the average citizen of America, as we, the average, usually don't even have the money to hire one good lawyer, much less half a dozen. We saw what it done in the Simpson case, a guilty person got off because of his ability to hire so many top notch, high dollar lawyers. The financial status of anyone should never interfere with justice, but by continuing the practice of more than one lawyer at a time, the financial status will continue to burden the justice system, as it always has in the past.

The judicial system is never held accountable for their actions or their decisions.

Sentences vary a great deal for the same crime, it seems to depend on financial status.

Sentences may be served or excused in leiu of probation, depending on the judge.

Offenders, unless life without parole or death penalty, never serve their full sentence.

Criminals are released from prison early and often repeat crimes against society.

Judges, lawyers and parole boards who turn known criminals loose on society should be, held accountable for their actions.

Judges, lawyers and parole boards should be held as direct accessaries to the next crime, that a released felon commits.

Judges or Parole Boards are Not Affected by Decisions they make.

This is because they are not held accountable for their actions.

Judges (due to psychologists interference) have greatly increased children's rights, but, difficulties for the parents, arising from those rights, are accountable to the parents, not the judges, lawyers, and certainly not the psychologists who started it all.

Accountability would probably decrease corruption. If a judge is offered a bribe, he or she, might think twice if he or she were held accountable for the next major crime committed by the person or persons, who gave the bribe. Example: If the mafia offered a Judge a bribe, and he took it, the judge might think twice if he or she were held accountable for the next mafia crime.

Judicial system is never held accountable for actions or decisions

Sentences can vary greatly for the same crime, it just depends on who you are and how much money you have. It also depends on how many attorneys you can hire for your defense, if you hire the right, and number of attorneys, a great deal of the time, you will be proved innocent, whether you are or not. (OJ Simpson, prime example) Had a poor or non-celebrity committed this same crime, they would have, I am sure been found guilty, and either got the death penalty or life without parole. Regarding the Simpson case, I have never figured out why the prosecution did not bring in several DOG experts, not just one, but a bunch of experts. His wife had an Akita, which is one of the most protective dogs in the world, had the dog not known who was attacking her, I believe he would have most definitely attacked the murderer, or murderers. The reason I say this is because I owned one, and anyone who has raised one, knows the dog would have attacked unless he was restrained in some manner, by a second person, and released after it was over, as the dog is the one who brought attention to the murder. This case is a prime example of our corrupt un-just system, and how finances play a huge role.The reason the dog did not attack is because he new the perpetrator, or perpetrators, or was restrained, one or the other.

Sentences can be served or excused, it all depends on the judge.

I believe our judges think they are GOD's, what right do they ever have, when they can over turn a sentence given by a jury? Defendants who ask for a jury trial do so for a reason, if they wanted to leave their sentence, or their lives, strictly up to a judge, they would not ask for a jury trial. One of the most bizarre cases of this in-justice, is regarding the case against a baby sitter,

Louise Woodward, who was sentenced by a jury, and the judge over-rode the jury, and only gave her time served, 9 months. I will always believe she did kill the child, and so does most of us. The childs parents, like any one of us, was and is still horrified, by that damned judge. Our system has got to change. A trial by jury is just like a vote by the people, and should never be changed by any person, this is another reason our system is corrupt.

Offenders who do not serve their full terms.

Now, this is a daily thing, for a person who commits rape, or child molestation, or any other crime, other than murder, theses offenders only serve a small portion of the time given to them by a jury. The justice system tells us it because the prisons are so over crowded, well if that is the case, why don't the system put to death all those who are on death row, and have been there for years, and years, and years. It is because our justice system has failed society. A person who has committed murder should only be allowed ONE appeal, and if that don't work in his or her favor, then they should be put to death immediately, not sit on death row for 20 years at the taxpayers expense. This would free up a lot of space in the prison's so that the other offenders could serve their real time. And plea bargains should be totally out-lawed. If you do the crime, be prepared to do the real time. Plea bargains are another reason we have corruption in the justice system. Charles Manson is the best example of our corruption, he is the perpetrator of the murders of many innocent people, and that asshole is still living in prison, at the taxpayers expense, he began the conspiracy involving his little idiots, who by the way are also still in prison, at the taxpayers expense, so why then are they not all, and should have been in the 1960's, put to death. Every state in the union should have the death penalty. Of course, we have all the liberals and bleeding hearts in America, who say NO, there are also innocent people in prison, to this I say, GOD takes the innocent along with the guilty, does he not? Every time the world has a disaster, flood, earthquake, volcanic eruption, hurricane, tornado, tsunami, GOD does not just take a portion of guilty or sinners, he takes the innocent as well, and maybe the reason for this is because they are too good for the world we live in today, so he is calling them back unto himself. So, if you are one of the better-than-thou, maybe you should think about that.

Criminals who are released from prison early often repeat crimes against society.

This is another daily occurrence, instead of serving their full sentences, they are released back onto society, back into the streets, to molest another child, or rape another woman, or hold up another gas station, etc. etc. etc. This is when I get really angry, at child molesters, and rapists. I believe the only way to put a stop to this is CASTRATION. If a man gets found guilty of either of these crimes, he should, upon his first day in prison, be castrated. At least then, and only then, would he be able to return to society, after his sentence is served, without society having to be frightened to death to allow their children to go outside, and women afraid to be out after dark I have been called a radical for feeling this way, but, I am not a radical, I am just using common sense, which our justice system does not have. The laws should be drastically changed in the law schools as well as in Congress, to protect society from rapists, murderers, and child molesters. When the justice system releases these men, it becomes dangerous to us all. This is when the judges, defense lawyers and parole boards, who turn known criminals loose on society, everyone of the people responsible for the release, should have to serve the time that the criminal got in the first place, tell you what, it sure as hell would stop wouldn't it? But only if that criminal did another crime. Our justice system really SUCKS.

Judges or Parole Boards are not affected by decisions they make.

The reason for this is first of all they are never held accountable for their actions, any more than the cold blooded murdering federal agents are. It is absolutely no skin off of their noses if they release a prisoner and he goes out and don't just rape a woman, or molest a child, but now he kills them. Too bad, so sad, but they don't give a damn. If, here again, the judge and every one on the parole boards were to be held as accessaries to the crime, and serve the maximum time, as an accessary. Sounds pretty harsh doesn't it? It is and it should be, to teach these high and mighty judges and parole boards, that we, society, are fed up with the release of these criminals, who only do 1/3rd, or less, of their time. Our justice system really SUCKS, at every level. Accountability would greatly reduce corruption, and we have a bunch of corruption in government and the justice system, from the police force all the way to the presidents.

The government and the state employees are not held accountable for the money they spend, which is our tax dollars. All the agencies make sure they spend ALL their budgeted amounts so that the following year their budgets will not be decreased. What these agencies do is, spend all the money they can at the end of the fiscal year, buying items or giving bonuses, which are not justifiable. Our tax dollars at work, right? If these agency employees were responsible for these budgeted monies and over-budgeted excesses had to be made up out of their own salaries they would certainly think twice before spending money frivolously.

Legislators, and lobbyists make and write the laws that we have to abide by, those voting for or against a bill must be held accountable whether they remain in office, or be voted out of office. The best example I can think of right now is the " burning of Yellowstone National Park", government ordered, " Let it burn" policy.

I ask you, has any government official, or any judicial body, been held accountable for any of their actions?

NOT Ronald Reagan for allowing Yellowstone to burn!!!!

NOT the parole board, who paroled a psycho, to kill again!!!!

NOT the Judge, who issued probation instead of time!!!!

NOT the District Attorney who accepted a plea bargain!!!!

ETC. ETC. ETC.!!!!

Government accountability has failed the American taxpayer since the beginning, but it began getting much worse in the early 1900's. With the formation of the F.B.I. in 1908, was not too bad until 1924, when J. Edgar Hoover took over as director, and from 1924 until his death in 1972, it became a real corrupt agency. And still is today. When the agents can kill in COLD BLOOD, and not be held accountable, and being paid by tax dollars.

EXAMPLE: We all know what happened at Ruby Ridge, but before most of us were born, back in 1934, another was shot in cold blood by an F.B.I. agent, and that was 30 year old Charles "Pretty Boy" Floyd, a bank robber, during the great depression.

The reason I even know anything about Charles Floyd, (the same with Bonnie and Clyde), is that my father, who was born in String town, Okla. In 1913, in his late teen years, rode the freight trains between Oklahoma, and Texas, he was a bronc buster for the King ranch is south Texas, so he did hear and see quite a lot in his travels. According to my dad, he was at a little hamburger joint, somewhere in Texas, sitting outside at a table, when a car pulled up, he said he knew immediately who it was, but kept his head down. When the car left, he said, Clyde Barrow, put his head out the window and yelled, "Call the Law, Bonnie and Clyde are in town." My dad said they spun gravel everywhere. This is the only time he ever saw them, but he said he respected them, as they helped the poor an awful lot, by bringing food or money and they hated the banks for all the farm forclosures. Bonnie and Clyde were killers, but how many bullets does it take to kill someone, they were riddled to bits, 20 miles from where my dad was living at the time.

In the case of "Pretty Boy" Floyd, my dad said he was a good person. My father was on his way from Oklahoma to Texas, when he hopped a freight train at the age of 19, this is in 1922. He caught the train and climbed into a boxcar, there were two men in the boxcar sitting at one end of it, they greeted my dad as he entered, my dad sat at the other end of the car, and daddy said the two men were talking so he would just look up once in a while and staying quiet. At one point when he looked up he spotted a pearl handled gun and that is when he knew who they were. He said he got pretty damned scared but he did know that Floyd was not a killer, just a bank robber, but he was still scared. After he saw the gun, he guessed Floyd knew he saw it as "Pretty Boy" Floyd got up and came over next to my dad and sat down. He said to my dad "you know who I am don't you?" and my dad said "yes, you're "Pretty Boy" Floyd, I saw one of the pearl handled guns." Daddy said at that point that he and Floyd began to talk and as they talked Floyd showed him his matching pearl handled guns. My dad said they were the prettiest guns he had ever seen. As they conversed, Floyd asked dad where he was from and daddy said String town, Floyd told him he was from Hanson, he asked my dad what he did for a living and daddy told him he broke broncs for the King ranch and worked out of Brownsville. My father left the train before Floyd and his partner, and never saw him again, all he could say about Floyd was that he liked him, that he was very well mannered, soft spoken, and seemed to be on the religious side, to an extent.

Per the biography channel, Floyd did try very hard to go straight after a 3 1/2 year sprint in prison, but (just like today) he was unable to maintain a job, as because every time a crime was committed here came the law, they harassed Floyd on every job he got, eventually after losing the jobs he desperately wanted in order to live a normal life, and found that this was damned near impossible to do, if it wasn't the cops, it was the depression and jobs were real hard to come by. I will always believe that if the cops had not harassed him,(and a lot of others) he would have been a very good citizen. They left him with no option, he had no where to turn except to crime, so he began robbing banks.

On October 22, 1934, "Pretty Boy" Floyd was killed in COLD BLOOD, by an F.B.I. agent, per biography channel, he was running across a corn field that had been harvested in the summer, so he had no cover to hide in, with the F.B.I. agent was a marksman, armed with a rifle, he first shot Floyd in the arm, Floyd dropped his gun, never even tried to return fire, then the marksman shot Floyd in the leg, he said on TV that he did not want to kill Floyd, just stop him. As he and the F.B.I.

agent walked up to where Floyd was lying, still very much alive, the agent took out his gun and shot Floyd in the head, killing him instantly. The marksman was quite surprised at this action, and the agent told him it was orders from HOOVER.

I used to think that any officer of the law or any agent from the many federal agencies we have, were better than the outlaws, but as you can see from the beginning, they are as bad, and in many cases, much worse. When it comes to the F.B.I. and the B.A.T.F. who is the criminal, the "Law or the Lawless?"

In 1924 J. Edgar Hoover became the Director of the F.B.I., and for 48 years ran a corrupt agency, no one ever being held accountable, for their actions.

Hoover, once John Dillinger was killed, trained all his attention on Charles "Pretty Boy" Floyd, and blamed every crime he could on Floyd in order to make him "public enemy # 1", Hoover did not care WHO committed the crime, and pursued no one for the crime, except Floyd. Consequently the real culprits went free. After Floyd's death, Hoover had the last of the so called "gangsters".

When Hoover became the head honcho of the F.B.I., organized crime bosses were elated, as they had Hoover in their hip pocket, because of gambling on the race tracks. He took absolutely no action on the Mafia or any organized crime families because he said there were no crime families or Mafia in America. How the hades did he know, as he was too busy betting the horses and cross dressing. Hoover was about the nearest nothing the F.B.I. ever had. It is very hard to believe he served as head honcho for some 48 years.

When John F. Kennedy became president and made Robert Kennedy (by the way, in my personal opinion Robert was the best of all the Kennedy boy's) the U.S. Attorney General, it became obvious to Hoover he better start acting like an F.B.I. Director. Because of Robert Kennedy's drive against the Mafia and all organized crime figures. Hoover became so scared of the Kennedy's, that he had their offices bugged. Why he was not terminated from his position, I believe, was because of Lyndon B. Johnson. (I will also always believe that Lyndon B. Johnson was behind the assassination of J.F.K., through organized crime bosses.)

The F.B.I. and the I.R.S. cannot be BUCKED by anyone, even the White House, and this has been true since the formation of both. We, the citizens, are in deep Do-Do, as we do not have one politician in Washington D.C. who has the BALLS to fight them or their corruption. Our politicians are corrupt so where does that leave us, the paeons. All that matters to the politicians is big business, OIL companies, BANKS, speaking of banks, next chapter, Americans in debt.

What the Federal Government has done, in fact, is create agencies that they cannot control, and are UN-TOUCHABLE, by government or the people. The F.B.I. (I guess that is why J.F.K. could not get rid of NUM-NUTS, J Edgar Hoover, the F.B.I. was and is untouchable, just like the I.R.S., and now the B.A.T.F.

Will there be no end to federal agencies, who control our every movement. From what I understand, even the cellular phones have chips in them that tell of our every movement. DO WE STILL LIVE IN AMERICA, OR HAVE WE, WITHOUT OUR KNOWLEDGE, SUCCUMBED TO A WORLD WE KNOW NOTHING ABOUT. TO BE RULED BY GOVERNMENT POLICE, AND CORRUPT POLITICIANS?

The justice system has made things so very complicated that any person who is being tried for a crime is told by the court that he, or she, must be defended by a lawyer. If you insist on defending yourself, the courts do not ever take into consideration that you may have enough common sense and possibly book learning to do so. There are an awful lot of folks in this country who would rather defend theirselves, than put their fate in some lawyers hands, at a tremendous expense. If a person does insist on his own defense, it really angers the ole judge, and 9 out of 10 times the defendant is shut up or found in contempt of court so many times that he or she gives up and does hire a lawyer, not by choice but necessity.

There is another place that the justice system has gone way too far, it is the raising of our children. The government has taken ALL control away from the parents. They are so concerned with child abuse that what they have done to the good parents in this country is atrocious. They have caused the children to become extremely non-respectful of all people, seniors, teachers, parents, and the rest of society.

There has from day one, been child abuse, in one form or another, and in the 1920's it was done by our own state governments, in state orphanages, detention centers, and allowed in schools with correction equipment such as wooden paddles with holes in them, even I had this experience in my schools in the late 1940's. Child abuse will never stop, no matter how many laws are passed, all the government has done is cripple the good parents, and there are by leaps and bounds, more terrific parents than bad parents.

There is a father, a single man, who lives on a ranch outside of the town I live in, Cody. He had at that time a son about 14 years old, if I remember right, anyway the son came home from school this one day (has to ride a bus) and his dad told him to do some of the chores, well the boy told his dad that he did not have to do anything that he didn't want to do. His dad asked him why he felt that way, the son told him that according to his teacher at school he did not have to do chores, or anything else that his dad told him to do. Well, I guess you know, that the father was just a little bit upset by this. The next morning he told his son to pack his suitcase and get ready for school, that he had to go into town for some seed and fertilizer and he would drive him to school. The boy asked why pack a suitcase, and the father said, you'll find out. Off they drove, into town, the father bought what he needed and by that time school was in session so he took the boy to school, he got out of the truck, walked with suitcase in hand, into the boy's classroom. He set the suitcase down next to the teachers desk and when the teacher asked what it was all about the father replied, "you told my son that he does not have to do anything I say, no chores, or anything else, so here is his clothes, you raise him and see if you can do a better job." The father then turned and left. I don't know what happened, I can just imagine that the teacher took the boy home to his dad, apologized to the father, and stayed out of everyone's family business after that. Working, doing chores at home after school has always been done by all families, but the government has made it very difficult for the parent to enforce any work from any child, and a little hard work has never hurt any of us. This true story happened in the early 1990's.

The story about the father, son, and the school teacher is a prime example of the loss of respect for parents that children of today have, and the system of government is to blame, with all the lobbyists in Washington for childrens rights, I think we are raising a bunch of heathens with absolutely no respect for anything or anyone.

Something happened to me last year that makes me believe this. I was sitting in my living room watching T.V., I have 3 Chow Chow dogs and they were with me inside the house when all at once they began barking, I got up and looked out the window, there was this dog on my front lawn that I had chased away several times before but he would not stay away from my yard. I looked to the street and there was a boy about 9 years old standing there waiting for this dog to get through pooping on my lawn. At this point I went outside and asked the boy to please keep his dog off my lawn. Well all hell broke loose, this boy started yelling and cussing at me, using curse words that I had only ever heard in a bar, I was dumbfounded, but then I got angry and started toward him, at that point we were both loud and he was still cussing me and then he reached down and picked up some rocks and threatened to throw them at me. Well, needless to say, that just made me more angry and I headed straight for him, I told him to go ahead and throw the rocks, but if I get my hands on you they will be the last rocks you ever throw. About that time a light blue van pulled up at my mailbox, about 50 feet away, the side door was slid open, the dog jumped in and the boy ran to it. A woman was driving the van, turned it around and went down the street. I called the sheriff and they sent a deputy out to my house, he took a statement, and after about 30 minutes he returned, said he found the boy at home, talked to his mother and at that time I found out that the boy was 8 years old. The deputy said the boy would be apologizing to me for the incident. About a week later the boy did so. Luckily I have not had any more trouble with this kid, but his dog is still running in my yard sometimes. After talking to another of my neighbors, she was telling me that the boys parents have 5 children and they are all in her words "brats" and the parents think their kids can do no wrong and are never punished in any way. The neighbor that told me about the family lives just across the street from them, and her husband is a preacher, so I do think she was telling the truth. As a matter of fact, I know she was, after all the cussing I heard out of an 8 year old.

The government has taken all power away from the parents when it comes to child rearing, so it is no wonder that children are what they are today. They have no self respect and respect for no one else. A good spanking on the rear end certainly never hurt me, and I got a few as I was growing up.

I had a friend when I was about 6 or 7 and my mom gave me a spanking one day for something, and afterward my friend told my mom, "I wish my mom loved me as much as you love Sheron" my mom asked her what she meant by that, she told mom that if her mother loved her maybe she would get a spanking when she did something wrong but her mother would not spank her for any reason. A puppy has to be taught from the git go, and so do children, a dog will only mind you if he has been taught to do so, and children are the same. A child is not born as an intellect, but has to be taught. The teaching begins at home, by the parents.

CHAPTER EIGHT

THE AGENCIES OF THE FEDERAL GOVERNMENT

▬ ▬ ▬ ▬ ▬ ▬ ▬ ▬ ▬

W E, AT LEAST MOST OF US, KNOW THAT THE AGENCIES OF the government are out of control, they spend our tax dollars so ridiculously.

Agency employees who earn a high wage, have every benefit, office, lab, etc. etc. for one very ridiculous example, testing the flow of Ketchup. Can you just imagine that if they are doing this, how many more really dumb things they are doing with our tax dollars.

And why are the taxpayers paying for oversea's advertising for the large corporations of the United States? Is this legal? I believe this is what may be called "Pork Barreling" by some of the good ole boy's who have been in the Congress for far too many years. These politicians probably got in a back room somewhere, had a few cocktails, smoked a few cigars, and decided the American taxpayer could afford to pay the bill. This came out on the C.B.S. news broadcast with Connie Chung, it was on the "Eye to Eye" news broadcast. She named Dole Pineapple, Gallo Wine" and more, I just cannot remember who the rest of them were. Well, I did not know I was paying for their ads oversea's did you?

And what about AREA 51, in the Nevada desert? This is supposed to be a Military highly classified, area. I was watching the T.V. I think it was on the History channel, recently and it was concerning Area 51. That there are billions of dollars spent yearly, but no one seems to know what on. Not even the President, so that should also tell us the government has agencies that it cannot control, and that are never held accountable, for tax dollars, or for anything else.

The Congress has so many lobbyist's in not only Washington D.C. but in every state congress as well, that the lobbyist's get things passed whether it be good or bad for the citizen's. A good example of this is the OIL companies. Supply and demand is the reason for the cost of diesel fuel rising, it is now higher than the premium gasoline price. It did not take the oil companies too long to figure out that so many diesel pick-ups were being sold, so the demand of diesel went to an all time high. What none of the citizen's thought about when buying these diesel rig's is that the trucking industry does in fact, MOVE AMERICA. As the price of diesel went to an all time high, it has cost everyone in this country more money to purchase any product, be it food, clothing, tires, auto mobiles, medications, it forced the price up on everything. It probably also caused an awful lot of independent drivers and small trucking companies to close down, as tires, diesel, food, everything cost more money, and after Sept. 11, everyone's insurance on their homes, went up. So, all you folk's who drive a diesel rig, (pick-up) do not scream about the price you pay for diesel, you brought it on all of us. I know you were not thinking about this when you purchased your diesel rig, but, there it is, Supply and Demand. The oil companies, like the banks, can charge whatever they want to charge, Congress de-regulated oil companies.

It is not only the diesel prices, but all oil prices have risen, the poor people are hit the worse, as with everything else, when the price of natural gas, propane, electricity, etc. goes to an all time high each winter, for home heating, and in the summer electricity goes to an all time high, for running an air conditioner. We, in the U.S. have several reserves of oil. During the 1970's when gas lines were all over the news, people waiting to purchase gasoline for their vehicles, is when things started, higher prices. During this time I went to California to visit a friend who lived in Martinez, and was amazed when he took me to the Suison Bay, which is just inland from the San Francisco Bay, and there were so many oil tanks, (those big round tanks that are used for oil storage) and he informed me that there was no oil shortage, that all the tanks were filled to capacity, and there were so many, I could not count them. According to Bob, it was just a way to scare the citizen's into paying more money to the oil companies for gas and oil.

The people around the world pay a much higher price for gasoline than (used to), however, they also have vehicles that get upwards of 150 miles per gallon of gas. Every time someone in this country comes out with a new carburetor that gets a higher mileage per gallon of gas, and from what I have been told, there have been a lot of them, they are bought by the oil companies. I have often wondered why the Automobile corporations don't come out with a car of truck that can get a much higher mileage per gallon, but maybe it is because the oil companies pay them not to. This is just my scenario, but there has got to be a reason.

We need the oil regulations put back in place by our government, or we will all be using horse and buggy's again. The poor will not have any choice.

E.P.A. & E.I.S.-These two agencies are I believe supposed to work together, however, I think they miss the boat most of the time. Example: In the 1990's highway work from the East entrance to Yellowstone began and was to be in 3 sections of 33 miles. The first 11 miles was from the entrance eastward, the second 11 miles was from the east of the end of project toward the center, (westward). The center 11 miles was to be done last, so as not to have heavy trucks on the newly built road. Regarding the first 11 miles, a company based out of Miles City, Montana got the bid. They began the job, and soon afterward they had to be closed down because of a FROG. The red spotted frog began their breeding season. So for two weeks, the construction workers could not work. I have to wonder what happened to the environmental impact statement regarding this red spotted frog. Did they not know of the frog's existence before the job began, or did they not care whether or not a family could be out of finances for that period of time?

I believe they did not care whether a man had a job or not, this is just one scenario regarding the E.I.S.. This sort of thing happens all the time all over the country. While the project was going on all the agencies were fighting and stopping the work, for one reason or another, and the construction crew's were just dumbfounded at how the Forestry, Wyoming Dept. Of Transportation, E.P.A., and the Sierra Club, all fought each other. While the agencies were fighting, stopping construction constantly, it became a real mess.

At that time I was a bartender, but the guy's would come in and tell me of the horror stories.

At this time, I, being a concerned citizen regarding the blundering of the agencies, called the Governor's office. The Governor, of course could not be bothered, so I was answered by an aide to the governor, Ken, a very nice young man and he transferred me to the office of the Wyoming highway Department. The head of the dept. was a very nice man, but he did argue with me about one thing, I told him that I believed the reason everyone was fighting is because each agency wants to be the BOSS, well he flatly denied that statement, that was, I believe on a Thursday, so when I got home on the next evening from work there was a message on my answering machine to call him the next morning. I called his home, and heavens to mergatroid, guess what he said ? He informed me that I was absolutely right, he apologized to me for arguing about it, and said he just could not believe the mentality of the agencies, and he would be in Cody that week, asked me if he could meet with me. We met, and he was very adamant about how he felt regarding the Forestry, E.P.A., E.I.S., & (the Sierra Club, on the top of his list)

Thanks to the men of Oftedal construction, and to the owner of Oftedal, along with the superintendents and foreman's of the job, in all the mess and fighting of the agencies, the job was completed on or before schedule.

The above is fact, and this happens every day of the week, somewhere in america. To men in the construction field. These agencies could care less if a man cannot work due to things like a red spotted frog, or like that certain kind of mouse in the Nevada desert. Do you remember though when the government employee's were laid off due to the government's budgeting problems? Well by damn those government employee's were constantly on the news networks and screaming and crying about not having their jobs, due to a temporary layoff. Not one government employee shives-a-git about the people they are responsible for getting laid off, but they cannot stand it if it happens to them. They proved that, did they not?

We need the E.P.A., however, they get too carried away in a lot of instances. We need people to care about the mother earth, as we all should do. We, most of us anyway, know that Hillary Clinton will no doubt run for the Presidency in the next couple of years, if she does so, I think she will put Al Gore in as the head of E.P.A. If this happens, he will be protecting everything from a mosquito or nat, to a grasshopper. Al Gore will get so carried away with the environment that we will probably all have to park our gasoline and diesel vehicles and buy electric vehicles. Dennis Weaver has an electric vehicle and is an environmentalist, but he does not carry things too far, by demanding that everyone else be like him. If Hillary does run, and gets elected, we had all better head for the high ground, as she believes that all women should stay home and bake cookies,(Marie Antoinette, let them eat cake) same reasoning isn't it? I would hope that the American citizens are going to get their heads out of the sand (Ostriches) and not ever elect Hillary Clinton for the Presidency, as she and Bill want to rule the world, that is why during Bill's presidency, many times they remarked about world power.

The E.P.A., it costs the people an awful lot of money if you are in business for yourself. I have a friend, Fred, in Sparks, Nv. He owns and operates a foreign car only, wrecking yard. He has fuel tanks in his yard, and when he purchased the business, any and all fuel tanks had to be underground. Years later here comes the E.P.A., and informed him he had to remove them and put them above ground. (note here: the tanks were at the beginning either on top of the ground or under the ground I cannot remember which, but the E.P.A. made Fred do the switch) He told me that it was going to cost him in the neighborhood of $20,000.00, this took place in the late 1980's.

The E.P.A., also came out with several new policies regarding the restaurant business. I, myself had an experience with the E.P.A.'s constant changing of their minds. I built a Club Casino in Reno-Sparks in 1986, bought all the restaurant equipment brand new from a restaurant supply house in Reno, at which time I purchased a brand new Hobart high temp dishwasher, and a medium size brand new grease trap. Within the first 2 years of business I was informed that I had to change the dishwasher to a Low Temp dishwasher and change the grease trap to a large capacity. Everything cost me more money, but in order to put in a larger grease trap, it meant cutting the concrete floor in order to make it fit, then putting down all new flooring around the new trap, and purchasing a new dishwasher. All this cost's money, but if you do not comply, they close you down.

The government agencies change their minds like we change underwear, daily and sometimes, twice a day.

The F.D.A., is another agency that cannot make up their minds. They will not legalize many drugs in this country because if it is not an american firm that came out with the new drug, then they will not approve it. So, what do citizens do? Go to Old Mexico, or to Canada, or to anywhere in order to be able to purchase them. In Old Mexico, the same drug that you can get in the states is so much cheaper, and it is the same drug, so everyone who can, goes there to purchase the products they need.

With the F.D.A., what was bad for us one day is good for us the next day. Is this sick, or do they just not know what the hades they are doing? The EGG, is the prime example. Do you remember when they told us eggs were bad for us? Then, here they go, and tell us they were wrong, eggs are good for us, as long as we don't eat too many. Well, people usually have eggs for breakfast don't they? I wonder how many is not good for us, as with breakfast, it is usually 2 eggs, at Easter we may eat 3 or 4 hard cooked eggs, and in potato salad there may be 3 eggs mixed in with everything else, but they are only trying to help us, right?

I do not know about you, but, every time I turn on my T.V. set there are drug ads up the ying-yang, and I have to wonder who in hades would ever take them, every one of the drugs advertised has so many side affects that the side affects would make you sicker than your problem. I guess the F.D.A., has made the manufacturers tell of all these side affects, whether they are true or not, so I cannot believe these drug companies can ever sell anything. I know I would not ever buy any of them.

We need the F.D.A., but they need to get their head out of the sand too.

Something extremely unusual happened to me yesterday, I normally do not ever turn on my T.V. until evening, but yesterday, after writing for about six hours, I turned it on at 3:30. This I have never done before, and I am so glad I did.

There was a paid program on a channel that I have never watched. But clicking through channels I, for some reason, stopped on this channel. Maybe it was because I am writing this book and was just on the section of the F.D.A. This author who has just completed a book on the F.D.A. was on talking about the drug companies and the F.D.A. I was extremely interested, so I watched it for awhile.

His book is named "Natural Cures They Don't Want You To Know About" and after listening to him discuss the drug companies and the F.D.A. I would suggest that everyone who has any kind of anything wrong with them should buy his book as he is saying that everything has a natural cure, no one needs drugs. I believe this is very true.

My sister has told me that her doctor's have done nothing for her except to keep prescribing drugs for her health problems. I have already told you that every time you see an advertisement on T.V. it is either about a mortgage company trying to get your home mortgage to pay off credit card debt, and if it isn't a mortgage company, it is drugs that make you more sick than you already are.

What is really bad is all these diet "WONDER" pills that they push to the max. I believe if a person needs to lose weight, they should stop eating so much, and stop eating foods that are bad for them, and exercise.

In his book he talks of obesity, diabetes, cancer, arthritis, migraines, herpes, and a lot more that are very curable without drugs, but rather cure yourself with vitamins and herbs. He said that the F.D.A. has been trying to list vitamins as drugs, and that they are trying to list everything as a disease. How sick is that? Our tax dollars at real hard work, right? Tax and the American Slaves are paying for all of this bogus BULL and why does the F.D.A. agents walk around with GUNS? So the taxpayers can spend more money on useless items for a federal employee, that's why.

His book is a must buy. "Natural Cures They Don't Want You To Know About"

CHAPTER NINE

BANKS AND CREDIT CARD DEBT

▬ ▬ ▬ ▬ ▬ ▬ ▬ ▬ ▬

THE DOWNFALL BEGAN IN 1950 WHEN THE DINERS CLUB put out plastic cards to be used for dining purposes in about 27 restaurants in New York City. These were the very first credit cards issued in the U.S.A. In 1951 the Diners Club came out with the credit card, and that is what they called it, a CREDIT CARD.

The first bank card was entered into our lives in 1958 by Bank of America and American Express. By the 1960's more and more banks became involved with the credit card, at this time the oil companies became involved, then the large department stores, Sears, Wards, etc. and today we have a credit card for every department store in the U.S.A., Wal-mart, K-Mart, Osco drug stores, Walgreens, Cost-Co, Home Depot, etc. etc. etc.

When the Oil companies began sending out credit cards they were not too bad as they kept them at a low credit line, this must have been in the 1960's, as far as I can remember most of the gas cards began with a credit line of $500.00 to $1000.00. At that time at least they were reasonable. Per the Encyclopedia Britannia the use of credit cards began in the united states in the 1920's, when individual companies, hotel chains and oil companies began issuing the cards to customers for purchases made at their businesses.

I suppose the beginning of the great credit card is not so important, what is important is that today, and since the late 1980's or maybe even sooner than that, the late fees and penalties are at a maximum.

American Express and the original Master Card, (now being MasterCard) had such a huge success that in the 1970's Congress began to regulate the credit card Mongrels by banning them for mailing out vast amounts of active credit cards to citizens who had never asked for a credit card. They were even sending credit cards to children, very young toddlers, and even to the family dog, probably the family cat and bird too.

The banks and credit card issuers wanted the entire American populace to get in, and stay in, the credit card scam. Well, they got their way, as most of America's populace has an average of 10 credit cards, and I have seen some people with as many as 20 different credit cards.

At some point, some legislators, thought very hard about making credit cards illegal, and there were a lot of critics that wanted very badly for Congress to outlaw the credit card..

Maybe the credit cards would have been outlawed if the banking industry didn't carry so damned much weight in this country, and it is so sad to know that the American people have a higher credit card debt than anywhere in the world.

A friend of mine was telling me a story about when his daughter entered college, she graduated high school the youngest of her class, due to her date of birth, she was 17 years of age. When she entered college she was still just 17, and here came the credit cards, in her mail. She called Terry, her father, and asked what she should do, use them or throw them away. Well, Terry, being a pretty smart guy, told her to max every damned one of them out, she asked him why, he informed her they could not collect the debt incurred because she was under age and they had no business sending her the credit cards until she reached the age of 18 years old.

The above story is true, and how many of these bad debts that are charged off does it take to get the credit card companies to wise up? They don't really care, as the interest and penalties of others more than make up for it, so they just continue to send cards to everyone, of age or not.

The credit card debt in America is so high that every time you turn on the Television set there is an advertisement for help with your debt, Dietech is constantly trying to get people to refinance their homes, pay off that high credit card debt, and cut the cards up. Well, we all know what is going to happen right? They will pay off the credit card debt, which is GREAT, but then here come all the new credit card offers in the mail, and it starts all over again. If you do not falter and fall right back into the cesspool of credit cards you will eventually come out ahead of the game, however, the mortgage companies, and the credit card companies know all too well that 99% of the public will go right back into debt with the credit cards, hell, that is what they are counting on. Now you will owe more on your home, and be right back into the credit card game too.

The only way to be free is to get a credit card counseling service, cut up the cards and don't ever accept another one. That is just exactly what I had to do, and no one could run fast enough to ever give or issue me another credit card. There was an excellent article in the April,2005, AARP monthly Bulletin, regarding the credit card issue. It was under the SCAM ALERT, and as I read it, I learned a whole lot more than even I ever dreamed possible regarding the interest rates and what happens if a payment is even one hour late. The article does say that in late fees alone the credit card issuers collected over $14.8 billion dollars. No wonder they don't care if a college student is old enough or not, with that kind of "LATE" fees only, and the principal on those credit cards was not even touched, they do have quite a scam going.

The government just thought that the Mafia, Costra Nostra, and organized crime syndicates, were bad for the American people, but all of them put together could not even come close to matching the scams of the banking and credit card industries. I will say again, who is the "law-less" a Mafia group, or the banking industry?

In my opinion, the banking industry is far worse for the American public than any organized crime unit. At least, for the most part, the Mafia, etc. leave the average citizen alone, and tend to their own business, unlike banks and credit card issuers,who, involve every American citizen in the U.S.A., even teenagers. And now, even if a person has to file bankruptsy because of credit card debt, our government has made it super hard for a citizen to even do that. So that tells us that our government must be in cahoots with the banking industry and the credit card issuers.

I.R.S. has very high interest and penalties, but even those asses cannot hold a candle light to the credit card issuers. I believe that the Government is not the only one who wants to BREAK the American people, so do the banks and credit card companies.

It is a very sad day when our government can stop kids from smoking, demand we wear seat belts, make the car companies build automobiles that are safe for us, make the car companies put the air bags in the cars to try and prevent injury in case of an accident, but where is the government safeguards for preventing injury by credit card companies and the banking industry? Mental stress is also a health problem, and with the high interest and high penalities, if you are even one hour late with your credit card payment, the mental stress will eventually take hold.

As soon as a child enters college here come the credit card issuers, knowing damned good and well that the college student, (who always needs money) will max the card out, and pay for it for the next 10 years, as the minimum payment on the card is only the interest, and a college student cannot afford any more than minimum, if that much. And it is not only the students that fall into the credit card TRAP, but 98 % of the American public.

The credit card issuers, regardless of which bank or company, has about the biggest scam in America going. They keep the cards limits up very high, a limit can be as high as $20,000.00 and in some cases, I'm sure, higher even. Hell's Bell's you could make a down payment on a house on some of the limits, but guaranteed, if you do make that down payment on a credit card, you certainly won't ever get the down payment paid, much less any of the rest of it.

If a person is late, even one minute late with a credit card payment, per the AARP bulletin, you can now be having to pay more interest rates on more than just the credit card. This is the latest punishment, called "universal default" and if you are late getting your credit card bill paid, your insurance, mortgage or auto loan rates can also increase. In some cases, if you are an hour late, whether it be the sometimes slow mail, or whatever reason, your credit card interest rate can triple. A single late payment can raise auto insurance rates as much as 50%.

The credit card issuers have started something else as well, like waiting before they send you your bill, this is just so you will be late and they can collect a shit-pot full of more penalties and triple the interest rates. The only way a person can safeguard against the tyranny of the credit card issuers is to make sure you make your payments at least 10 days in advance. I am not sure but you might be better off just paying on-line, I don't know that much about paying bills on line, so if you decide to do that, find out about it first.

Where in the HELL is the intervention by the federal government, this is TYRANNY.

The federal government, F.B.I. and the U.S. Attorney's Office are always after the so-called organized crime families for one reason or the other, one of the reason's is called "Loan Sharking" and this is a felony, correct?

The straight facts are, the Banking Industry or any other industry who distributes credit cards, previously mentioned Dept. Stores, etc. etc. And their bank's location is in one of the following states, Arizona, Delaware, South Dakota, New Hampshire, Utah, or Virginia, according to the interest rates they are allowed by law to charge, are nothing more than "Legal LOAN SHARKS" and the murder they commit is not with a gun, but nevertheless, only because you are still breathing, after the peril of a Credit Card disaster, you may as well be dead, as you will never get out from under the banking loan sharks, as they have killed your credit rating, whether it be your fault or not. Slow mail contributes, and sometimes even a Consumer Credit Counseling agency may not get your payments to the bank on time, so, whatever the reason, if your payment is late, you are up shit creek without a paddle.

The so called "Loan Sharking" is now a LEGAL business, IF it is done be a BANK. I believe that the organized crime syndicates should go into the banking business, at least then they would be "Legal Money Lenders", which, is the same as a "Loan Shark." If the Mafia quit doing whatever it is that they do and began building or buying banks they would get BILLIONS of dollars every year just for late payments, and the principal on the credit cards would never be touched. GREAT RACKET right, and it is LEGAL.

If the Mafia went into the banking business and began to issue credit cards, like the rest of ALL the banks, HELL they would not have to do anything else, and they would become "UNTOUCHABLE" by the FEDERAL Government or anyone else. The government, state and federal have given the banking industry the right to ROB the citizens blind without a GUN.

Gee, it's too bad we can't all own a bank, that way we could issue each other a credit card and legally rob each other. This kind of tells us why Jesse James, the Dalton Gang, Bonnie and Clyde, Charles "Pretty Boy" Floyd, and all the rest of the bank robbers of the past did rob banks. The banking industry must have always robbed the POOR, LEGALLY.

I Believe that it is the responsibility of the State Governments, ALL of the states in the U.S.A. that should be held accountable for the credit card run-a-way interest rates. They are the ones that should put a cap or ceiling on the "out of control" high interest rates by the credit card issuers, ALL of the issuers.

It is the State governments that do not put a cap on interest rates regarding credit cards. It is the federal government which has allowed the banks to carry on an illegal "LOAN SHARKING" business. If loan sharking is illegal, why do all the banks or any credit card issuer get by with it?

The banks target low income and lower middle class citizens for their "TYRANNY"

Every defense attorney in America who goes into court to represent anyone who has been charged with "loan sharking" should let it be known to the court, that if the banking industry can be "legal loan sharks" through charging whatever interest rate they choose, or put as many penalties on a credit card consumer that it wishes, then it is no different than any ordinary citizen who loans money and charges a high interest rate on the loan. It is legal for banks, so why not everone else? Is there a double standard here?

In 1996 we, the people, were really screwed over again by the U.S. Supreme Court, (nothing new is it?) Prior to 1996, the federal government had restrictions on credit card late penalty fees. In 1996, the U.S. Supreme Court lifted those restrictions, because of this action the bankers, ALL the bankers, became legal "LOAN SHARKS". We, the people, must have a bunch of either bought and paid for Supreme Court judges, or they just don't give a damn, or they just do not have any COMMON SENSE, AND BECAUSE OF THEM, WE, THE PEOPLE, HAVE NOW GOT BANKING "tyrants", WITHOUT ANY LIMITS.

There is now "NO LIMIT" on the amount that a bank can charge a cardholder for being even an hour late with a payment. It is not only loan sharking, but TYRANNY, by the banking industry. Without any Federal controls, and without higher controls by the States, we are SUNK.

In the case of the State's, there are "usury laws" that are either very weak or non-existent, so the credit card issuers moved into these states in order to have "legal loan sharking". The following states have either no caps, or very weak caps.

ARIZONA-36% cap (weak) Bank of America and Direct Merchants
DELAWARE-NO CAP- J.P. Morgan Chase, M.B.N.A., Morgan Stanley Discover, H.S.B.C.
NEW HAMPSHIRE-NO CAP- Providian
SOUTH DAKOTA-NO CAP- Citibank
UTAH-NO CAP- American Express
VIRGINIA-NO CAP- CAPITAL ONE

These clusters were formed by a 1978 Supreme Court Decision (supreme court again) that determined National Banks only have to obey the interest-rate caps of the state they are chartered in, not that of a state where a banks customer lives. This means that when a bank from a state without limits on interest (above states) issues credit cards to people living in states like Minnesota, which caps credit card interest at 18%, the customer can be charged any rate of interest.

After learning about all this, I have got to wonder who is really running America, is it our elected politicians, the supreme court justices, or is it the banking industry? At the present time, I believe it must be the banking industry, they are "TYRANNOUS" and the government will not stop it, so that is why I believe the banks are running America. I also believe they are trying hard to completely break the American Citizen, with the supreme courts BLESSING.

Personally, I believe that credit cards should be totally outlawed, as not only do we pay a very high interest and penalty rate if we are late, but it is also a way for someone to steal our identity.

Identity theft has happened to millions of people in this coutry, and it will never stop as long as we have credit cards. The people who steal your identity can destroy you, not only with the heartbreak of not being able to get a new mortgage for a lower interest rate, but also the heartache of trying to get your credit rating back to normal, and in the process trying to prove that it was not you that ran the bills up.

I suggest that you do all your banking on-line so no one can steal your bank account numbers from your mailbox. Do not ever give your social security number to anyone except your employer, or other needful sources.

As I was working in the store one day a woman came in and bought a bottle of wine, as she came up and checked out she gave me a personal check, from a local bank and I immediately noticed that not only was her name and address and phone number on the check, but so was her social security number. I asked her about it, and told her I thought that was a very dangerous thing to do. She just said she thought it was a good idea to have it there. Now I have to wonder what bank would ever allow this. I wish I could remember what bank it was, I could find out why they would ever allow it to happen, even if the customer requested it, it is extremely dangerous.

A person who steals an identity can do so by stealing your mail, getting your business cards, getting your credit card number's off of credit card statements from the mail box, and by getting your A.T.M. pin number.

The same can be true of a debit card number, but most of us do not have thousands of dollars in our checking accounts, most of us keep a balance of under $1000.00 in checking accounts so a person who is into identity theft will mostly leave this area alone. Still, watch your account daily, and I repeat, do all your banking on-line, this will eliminate the mailbox problem, for the most part.

The mailbox has a big problem when it comes to the bank credit cards, as every day, today alone I had four new credit card offers in the mail, and this is a recurring nightmare with all of us. When they send these damned things out, it is not on anyone's request, they just send them, and if someone is watching your mail, they can take them, and call in and get the credit card issued, get the address changed, and there it goes.

I was watching a broadcast about identity theft, and the person was explaining that we should never give our mothers maiden name as well. She said there are too many ways to find out what it is, if they have your name, it is so easy to get your mothers name. She suggested you come up with a password, and never give it out, not even to your family members. There is one really good thing about credit unions your mail is not full of credit card offers.

It is my thought that if everyone who is dealing with a bank, be it a mortgage, credit card, or any kind of loan, he or she should find a credit union, pull any and all monies out of the banks, run, not walk, to the nearest credit union, and do the same business with them. Credit Unions are owned by the membership, for the most part a credit union will give a member a loan when they have been turned down by a bank.

This is not totally the bank's fault, as the Federal Government controls the banking industry while so far, they do not control the credit unions. About 8 or 9 months ago, Aug. or Sept. 2004 while making a deposit at my credit union, they were asking for signatures on a petition. It seems that the banking industry was losing so many customers to the credit unions that the banks was trying to get the government to regulate the credit unions just as strongly as they were regulating the banks. So far, they have not succeeded, and hopefully, never will.

Mortgage companies are your best bet for a home mortgage I believe, as the banking industry is getting very rich off of your credit card debt. So, if we, the citizen's begin a revolt against the banking industry by moving our monies and our loans, they might get the idea, and correctly so, that the American people are fed up with their "Loan Sharking Tyranny" regarding the credit card issue.

If your credit union issues credit cards, the smart move would be to get your card through them, as they are a Co-Op, and they are not listed in the previous states that have NO CAP, on interest rates. I honestly believe this is the only solution that will cause the banking industry to stop their tyranny of high interest rates. It is no wonder the bankers are so wealthy, sucking the blood of the citizens of America the way they do.

CHAPTER TEN

WRAP UP OF
PRECEDING CHAPTERS

— — — — — — — — — —

S LAVERY COMES IN MANY FORMS. THE BLACK AMERICAN'S were in bondage, some people are slaves to the husband, or to the wife, or to the children, in one way or another. But all American citizens are under a slavery of the Internal Revenue Service. We are all crooks and outlaws if there is any problem with our taxes, until we can prove them different, by hiring a C.P.A. or a high priced lawyer. Abolish the I.R.S.

The citizens who are drawing social security should be allowed to work all the hours and make all the wages possible that they can earn. If this were done, they would continue to pay into the social security program, which would be very helpful for later generations. Instead of putting the monies for the social security benefits into the lending or stock markets, it should be left alone, and take some of the I.R.S. employee's and put them to work in the Social Security Administration, where at least, they could help someone.

The government cover-ups are so many, and the cold blooded murder of citizens, especially during the first four year term of Clinton, Randy Weaver's ordeal and loss of family at Ruby Ridge, the disastrous firing upon citizens at Waco killing women, men and children, and the tragic bombing of the Murray building in Oklahoma City. These should never be forgotten any more than the Twin Towers on Sept. 11, 2000. The federal government knew of the Oklahoma City bombing in advance and they also knew of the Twin Towers in advance. Why then did they not do something about both? Because, we the people, are all expendable, and the powers to be think they are all Gods.

The State taxing system is something that every voter should be thinking about very hard. We are the only ones that can change it, by our vote. Only vote for someone who promises to fight against state income tax, and who promises to cut the high property taxes, as well as exempting food, clothing, drugs and non prescription drugs, footwear, home heating fuels and electric. If the human body has to have it to survive, it should not be taxed. Only vote for a candidate who will do these things. That is the only way we can change it. We also need the new politicians to lower the taxation on gasoline and diesel fuel, as we all need both for survival, seeing as how we all have to depend on our vehicles to get to and from work, just so we can pay all these taxes.

The trucking industry will always be the industry that moves America. With the d.u.i. laws we have today, a guy cannot even have 2 beers without being over the legal limit. Well this is asinine, but it is true. The truck drivers of America should have a C.D.L. license as well as a residential license, to always be able to protect his or her livelihood. I have been trying to get someone to listen to me for years regarding this issue, maybe someone somewhere, will do so.

The American justice system really did not need O.J. Simpson or Michael Jackson to make a mockery out of it, they helped a great deal, but our judges and our lawyers and the district attorney's offices all did it. They continue to do so. If you have money, and the more you have, the better off you are, anytime it comes to justice. People are always saying it is better than other countries, well that certainly don't say much for it, now does it? In America, you are guilty until you can prove your innocent. From what I have heard, Singapore has no crime. Maybe they have a good system, I don't know, just what I was told, by my sister who lived there for some time.

The agencies of the federal and state governments are out of control. The governments cannot control their own agencies. Now this is really bad for us poor paeons. The Sierra Club, and the E.P.A., are always coming up with a new environment control for us paeons to abide by, but what about the controls on our government, who is always bombing the hell out of something.

It is the governments of the world which are destroying mother earth, and ours is probably the worst of all of them. Remember that rare mouse in Nevada, well where does the government set off most of their bombs for testing? In the Nevada desert. Poor little mouse. They also set off the bombs in the ocean, what about the sea creatures that die? Well, where in the hades is the E.P.A. or the Sierra Club when this happens? They do not care because it is government, but don't cut that dead tree down, there is a spotted owl nesting in it, their mentality is the hell with the lumberjacks job, save that spotted owl. Maybe they all live in brick or adobe houses, no wood in their house, BULL. I say, it's alright to try to save the environment, but if that is what they are really trying to do, they need to start at the start place, government bombings, and missile target practice. Our Tax dollars at work, helping to destroy mother earth. One good thing about the Native American Indians, they protected the Mother Earth.

Regarding the banking business and the massive credit card debt of us paeons, we will pay and pay and pay, unless you RUN to your nearest Credit Unions, and stay there. They have credit cards as well, but not with the loan sharking interest and penalty rates. Not only that but when you go to a credit union, the building is usually small, no outlandish furnishings, just all business, not showing off how wealthy the credit union is. The banks, on the other hand, are huge, with fine furnishings, art up the cabuska, not cheap art either. Well, now you know where all that $14.8 billion went. The bankers live like kings while the credit unions are humble employees and we, the membership, don't give a hoot about fancy, just honesty and productivity.

Well Kids, I guess that just about wraps it up, you will have to make your own decisions on the things I have covered in the book, but one thing I hope you will all do is, VOTE THE LIFERS OUT OF OFFICE, until that is done, nothing will be done.

J.F.K. - Ask not what your country can do for you, but rather, what you can do for your country. Vote, and vote the lifetime politicians out of office, that is all we are capable of doing. Vote for smaller government, as ours is too big, and out of control, State and Federal alike.

CHAPTER ELEVEN

THE SUPREME COURT AND EMINENT DOMAIN

▬ ▬ ▬ ▬ ▬ ▬ ▬ ▬ ▬

I HAVE REPEATED OVER AND OVER AGAIN IN THE PRECEDING chapters that we have a government that is out of control, and that we have a government that does not give a hoot about the paeons of America, only the wealthy and the large corporations. The ruling of the supreme court on the eminent domain issue of Kelo vs. New London on Thursday June 23, 2005 is the best proof you will ever have of that fact, and that America is only for the rich and large corporations.

America is becoming more communistic each and every day. The supreme court's ruling is proof that the judges in this country, all judges, especially the supreme court judges, should be elected with limited terms in office, not appointed with lifetime service. No public servant should be appointed, they must ALL be voted into office with limited terms. For the sake of the future generations please get to the polls and VOTE.

The state governments should by all means take a stand and limit eminent domain to it's original purposes, military and highways, and by no means should a city or county government be allowed to take someone's property so as to sell that property to a giant corporation for more taxation.

Ralph Nader said it very plainly, there is NO common sense and that it tarnishes constitutional law. State courts remain free to impose more reasonable restraints on government taking of individual property.

A New York Times editorial supported the Kelo ruling, but all the letters the NY times published today were against it.

Here are some of those letters:

To the Editor:

Most of these corporations get tax breaks to build and develop in these areas. So what is the real return to the people of the municipality.

Karen Greene
New York, June 24, 2005

To the Editor:

The idea that local governments may seize people's homes and businesses for private development is directly in conflict with the found-

ing idea that the government is formed to en-
sure life, liberty and private property.

If indeed governments are given the power
to take from those who have established themselves, under the pretext of building something
"for public use" (which in reality is a private
development of sorts), it strikes me that private
developments, and not public ones, are being
supported in this ruling.

By the very nature of this decision, then,
doesn't this mean that local governments can
take people's lands for private use, rather than
for "public use"?

James Evans
New York, June 24, 2005

To the Editor:

Re: "The Limits of Property Rights (editorial, June 24):

Not mentioned in your editorial and news
coverage of the Supreme Court decision was a
crucial fact: the decision to raze a mixed-use,
mostly working class neighborhood in New
London was essentially dictated by the State of
Connecticut under Gov. John G. Rowland, not
freely chosen by the city.

Officials in the Rowland administration,
now notorious for its corruption, told New
London that the state would provide millions

of dollars for development in the Fort Trumbull neighborhood but that the city would have to go along with the plan, carried out by the New London Development Corporation.

Mr. Rowland was thus able to brag about bringing jobs to New London, while residents of the neighborhood paid the price: losing their homes.

If eminent domain is to continue, the decision must truly be made by local officials, those who have to look the dispossessed in the eye.

Philip Langdon
New Haven, June 24, 2005

To the Editor:

Regarding those being evicted, you refer cavalierly to those "who will, in any case, be fully compensated" (editorial, June 24)

How, may I ask, do you fully compensate an 87-year-old woman who is being evicted from the home in which she was born and in which she probably wanted to die?

I wonder if you will feel the same way when the government decides that it needs to evict you from your home with "full compensation."

Having been evicted from rentals because of change of ownership and condo conversions, I once believed that as an owner, I could at last be secure in my own home. Obviously, that is true only until such time as the government decides that it needs my home for the "public good."

Wendy Miller
San Rafael, CA. June, 24 '05

To the Editor, LA Times:

Ruling in Property Case Shows Poor Judgement

Re "Justices Back Forced Sale of Property, " June 24: The Supreme Court ruled that nice working-class homes—with their owners living there for decades—can be demolished to build for the high end market. It's bad enough that the housing boom is generating luxury houses and precious few affordable ones, and that rents have skyrocketed. But now even if you already own, the rich can take over your property if they like the view and have bought friends in government.

With decisions like this one form the Supreme Court, the American dream has been downgraded to owning your own tent.

Mery Lynn McCorkle
Los Angeles

To the Editor

I'm certain justices of the Supreme Court all have nice homes in nice neighborhoods. But wouldn't a city be better off building high-rise condominiums on those properties?

Mike Kapowich
Corona Del Mar

To the Editor, Minneapolis Star Tribune
June 28, 2005:

Robbed of A Dream—The American dream is to own your own house. With today's prices, that often means decades of work. You save and you pay and you work to own your own piece of Americana. We often forget that this opportunity can be taken away.

The Constitution of the United States contains in the Bill of Rights the concept of eminent domain—the idea that the government may purchase land at a fair price from individual citizens for those reasons deemed "in the public good."

Now the government uses this right for the building of corporate facilities. The government now tells its citizens they must move not for a school or road but for an IKEA or a WAL-MART. And last week, the U.S. Supreme Court upheld the right of local governments to engage in this practice.

I have to wonder if this is ever done to multi-million dollar estates or if only the homes and dreams of lower-income Americans are taken away. And is it not one underlying function of a government to protect the private property rights of its citizens? If so, does this not run counter to the fundamental job of our government?

This seems to be just one more encroachment of corporate greed and the government protecting the rich and powerful at the expense of everyone else.

Jim Timmerman
St. Peter, Minn.

I would like to say, this act by the Supreme (Beings) not justices in any manner of the word, should scare the hell right out of everyone who owns property anywhere near a pristine area of the country. I believe the ones who voted for this should not only resign their positions but should also be tarred and feathered and be forced to move to a communist country. They have put themselves above God and Country and they should be forced to resign.

If we have a Senator or a Representative in Washington DC with a hair on their ass they need to get busy and over-ride this decision by the Supreme Court Super Beings. This should be done now not 10 years down the road.

If you live in a state that petitions are allowed, get petitions signed by enough of the state's population to get the issue on the ballot, and vote it out. If you cannot get things on a ballot with petitions, call your Representatives and your Senators daily, and insist they vote public domain for nothing but needful uses.. If they do not, do not vote for them again, and the same goes for Governors. It's about time the American people stood up for the Pursuit of Happiness, Liberty, and JUSTICE.

The forgoing letters to the editor was an example of how all America feels over the Eminent Domain vote by the jerks who voted for it.

IT IS GOING FROM BAD TO WORSE IN THE U S A, AS HE WHO HAS THE MONEY TAKES THE PROPERTY.

When any politician can remove families from their homes to allow big business to move in just for tax purposes then why are they only charging $1.00 per year for rent on a 99 year lease? Where can the every day person go and pay $1.00 per year for rent on land? We cannot, now can we?

In this book I have written how bad our justice system is, and how we have a government that is out of control, this issue is just one example of how out of control things really are.

VOTE–VOTE–VOTE–VOTE–VOTE–VOTE–VOTE

This is the only way we can change things, vote for the poorest person running, not the rich kids, vote the lifetime politicians OUT of office, and lets get TERM limits set for ALL public office.

Until then it will not change----but just keep getting worse.